AS FOUND HOUSES

EXPERIMENTS FROM SELF-BUILDERS IN RURAL CHINA

APPLIED
RESEARCH
+DESIGN
PUBLISHING

JOHN LIN AND
SONY DEVABHAKTUNI

TABLE OF CONTENTS

Early twentieth-century European artists, notably Marcel Duchamp, discovered the eye-opening world of the "readymade" or "found object." These were quotidian things, untouched by artistic conventions: the bottle rack, the bicycle, the urinal.

That ordinary world is, of course, always there. It is where we live. But sometimes, our education in art and architecture makes the ordinary harder for us to see. Some people, including certain architects, were aware of the commonplace and found the ordinary extraordinary. One of these architects was Bernard Rudofsky, who in 1964 published his observations in *Architecture Without Architects*.

The question I have: Could a non-architect write a book on "non-pedigreed architecture"—as Rudofsky framed his subject? My answer would be no. Only trained eyes see architecture in everyday structures: the quality, creativity, and ingenuity.

In the work that comes together in *As Found Houses*, John Lin and Sony Devabhaktuni, two architects based in Hong Kong, have completed an architectural reading of 20 vernacular buildings in rural China. The black-and-white, axonometric, analytical drawing of each house translates the informal into the learned, without interfering with the original ideas of the self-builders nor projecting the self-consciousness of design. The naming of the houses constitutes another layer of analysis, which gives a conceptual clarity to the seemingly spontaneous constructions. Field research of this kind forcefully exercises architectural intelligence and may serve as a re-education for an architect. In late 1960s China, high school students were sent to the countryside to be re-educated by the peasants. In this volume, John and Sony send architects to the villages with some vital questions:

Are we not designing too much or are we designing for design's sake? Have we confined ourselves to a particular language or taste or way of thinking? How do we become freer? If *not to design* is not an option for architects, can design be without design?

Yung Ho Chang

The philosophy and know-how of the anonymous builders presents the largest untapped source of architectural inspiration for industrial man. The wisdom to be derived goes beyond economic and esthetic considerations, for it touches the far tougher and increasingly troublesome problem of how to live and let live, how to keep peace with one's neighbors, both in the parochial and universal sense.

Bernard Rudofsky, from the preface to the exhibition catalog for *Architecture Without Architects*, Museum of Modern Art, New York, 1964

Photo by Graf zu Castell-Rüdenhausen. Used with permission.

It is an image that captures the imagination through its obscurity: black squares receding on a bleached plane. Looking closer, the simplicity of the architectural forms reveal themselves to be courtyards dug in the ground. These courtyards lead to a series of hollowed out, arched spaces extending perpendicularly into the earth from their walls. These spaces would be used for living, sleeping, cooking, and storage.

An entire house built by excavation demonstrates the simple integration of the culture of courtyard living within the constraints of the only available building material: earth. A harmonious balance between agricultural production and communal living is reached through the division of farmland above and domestic activities below.

Several years ago, we decided to visit Sanmenxia in Shaanxi province where the photo was originally taken, wondering if we could find the exact site of the iconic image. Instead, we discovered a landscape of factory buildings sprawling between dug-out homes. The sites of vernacular architecture were being radically transformed as urbanization reached once remote areas. Many underground homes have been abandoned or are in a state of disrepair, with new homes being built above ground on what had previously been collective land. An ambiguous and contradictory landscape—of newly built generic houses, remnants of underground courtyards, sprawling factory buildings, and large-scale infrastructure cutting deep into the earth—has emerged.

Forces of urbanization have altered the delicate symbiosis in which dwelling exemplifies livelihood; today, this relationship clings to the vestiges of traditional living. Deng Xiaoping unleashed these forces when he announced his plans for Special Economic Zones in 1978. These policies opened China to the global market, eventually kick-starting the most rapid and widespread urbanization the world has seen. Although these initial policies focused on the creation of new urban areas and encouraged millions of migrant workers to abandon their villages in search of work in the cities, urbanization slowly and inevitably reversed course, invading the countryside.

It has been over 50 years since *Architecture Without Architects* introduced vernacular or "non-pedigreed" architecture to a wider audience. Revisiting Rudofsky's premise on vernacular architecture through the lens of contemporary China is to be confronted with abandonment, infrastructural collisions, mutations, adaptations, and contested territories: rapid urbanization either directly or indirectly impacting what was once far removed. What we find today are changing forms of livelihood, contrary to the isolated, and well-integrated settlements idealized in the exhibition and catalog. The "vernacular, anonymous, spontaneous, indigenous, and the rural," has to be reconsidered through a new narrative that accounts for the intrusion of global development on vast territories of land.

Recently, we began to ask ourselves, what *is* the vernacular today? As we witness millions of builders altering and adapting their traditional homes with industrial material, can we identify surprising and innovative solutions that suggest a new way of appreciating its meaning? We found some answers on our first journey to the dug-out homes in northern China. At the time, we met a family that had built a new house above ground but continued to live underground during the summer and winter months when the thermal insulation of the earth walls still offered comfort.

This back-and-forth movement revealed a transitional lifestyle that responded to the climate through a hybrid way of living. Instead of controlling the temperature with technology and energy, the simple change of aligning to the seasons led to a new understanding of what vernacular architecture could offer today—insight into wholly contemporary forms of living. We began to consider how self-made adaptations to traditional houses suggested novel approaches to important architectural questions, including, in this instance, how to live sustainably.

This initial observation led us to consider other sites of vernacular architecture throughout China. Were there more stories of contemporary living hiding in plain sight? Over the past five years, we have embarked on numerous journeys to discover and document cases of vernacular renovation, often bypassing well-preserved traditional houses in favor of ones that might otherwise seem compromised by additional construction. We traveled across the diverse climatic and environmental ranges of China, eventually focusing our attention on four regions where adaptations offered particularly strong lessons: the underground houses that were the starting point of the work; wooden houses of Dong minorities in China's mountainous south-central region; the large communal houses, or *tulou*, of southeastern China; and the high-altitude dwellings of the Tibetan people in the far west.

Through the study of these cases, we began to perceive the spirit of economy driving the rural builder: nothing is done which doesn't have a good reason or direct impact. A spirit of ingenuity couples industrial and traditional methods in a new functional dynamic that overrides formal design considerations. We adjusted our focus to appreciate the mismatched and often contradictory esthetics found in these renovated houses. Having been influenced by the cultivated imagery of an *Architecture Without*

Architects, we had to refashion our association of vernacular architecture with a powerful formal purity.

The spirit of learning from the vernacular—the essential meaning of Rudofsky's work—can still find a compelling argument today, pointing to the uncontested design aptitude of the untrained architect. As a contemporary design audience, as in 1964, we hope to find novel insights on present-day issues: the challenges posed by industrialization, environmental damage, infrastructural expansion, climate change, and population shifts. What new lessons can be learned from the "spontaneous" self-builder?

In southern Guizhou province and parts of Hunan, Yunnan, and Guangxi is the largest group of wooden house builders in China. Even though the craft and knowledge of wooden house construction are in decline, led by the profusion of concrete frame and brick, the wooden house displays a surprising resilience. In part, this can be attributed to the movable nature of the wooden house itself; the structure can be easily dismantled and put back together, making elements easy to reuse. We discovered many surprising combinations of newly-built concrete and brick structures that integrated pre-existing wood elements; elsewhere, we saw examples of entire wooden houses rebuilt on top of multistory concrete frame structures. The case studies demonstrate strategies for combining different structural systems. They point to an integration of traditional methods that creates an entirely contemporary idea of "house" where the recycling of the old arrives at something new.

Stories of structural adaptation often happen alongside social and community transformation. The large multi-family earthen houses of the Hakka people in southern China emerged hundreds of years ago in a fiercely combative culture. Extended families built thick earthen walls for collective defense, while maintaining a shared, central open space. Over time, as more and more of these *tulou* (the Chinese term for "earth house") dotted the landscape, new relationships began to form between them. Some *tulou* housed marketplaces or schools in central courtyards. A proto-urban condition emerged where collective spaces were not only used privately but as shared public institutions in an increasingly densifying region.

Today, the space between *tulou* has become cluttered with individual concrete and brick houses that occupy every piece of land. Sometimes, the *tulou* themselves are abandoned, their protective walls preserving what is often the only remaining open area within the village.

Each family traditionally lived in a vertical slice of rooms, accessed through a shared corridor and balcony. Therefore, the greatest limitation to living in the *tulou* was the difficulty of adapting or expanding the individual living units. Despite these constraints, we discovered that not all *tulou* families have dismissed the potential for collective living. Modern residents have found radical new ways to expand their home, either by directly plugging in structures from outside the earthen wall, or by rebuilding the *tulou* section by section with an individual style and layout that respects the collective footprint. These adaptations are not only physical but also transform the notion of cooperation. They represent a new commons: new reasons for living together that account for individual desires.

Around Xianggelila in western China, we looked at traditional Tibetan homesteads built with one-meter thick earthen walls. In the past, the forecourt enclosed by these walls was used for raising animals; the wall also comprised the outer limit of a two-story, pitched roof structure, supported by powerful wooden columns and beams. In recent years these robust dwellings have been transformed by additions that make use of readily available steel and glass construction. A decade ago, contractors would come from cities several hours away; today, materials and building know-how are accessible.

The new additions are often large enough to envelop the original earthen house and courtyard within the newly added shed. The resulting hybrid constructions—massive walls supporting a grid of steel and glass—are contradictory, but suitable for a high-altitude climate of frigid temperatures and strong sunlight. These structures have proliferated throughout neighborhoods in and around Xianggelila. New house constructions often incorporate the glass structures into their designs. In the evening, the urban landscape transforms from an ancient Tibetan town into a metropolis of glowing glass volumes.

The unrestrained manner in which local builders adapt hundreds-years-old structures demonstrates the vitality by which "design" remains as much a prerogative of the rural self-builder as the urban professional.

As evidenced in our journeys, it is still possible to perceive a singular defining quality among traditional and vernacular architecture: an evolution over time that leads to unbelievably diverse forms. In the past, this evolution resulted from a collective process of building that related to local materials and to techniques passed down over generations. This gradual process allowed for the maintenance of a perfect synchronicity between architecture and livelihood.

But what happens when change happens suddenly, creating a schism in the design of space and its capacity to enable a specific way of life? Our examination of the ways that local self-builders have adapted their houses to negotiate this schism reveals new ideas, but also an opportunity, inviting the architect to participate. The book presents new ways that the study of informal building can enlighten the formally trained designer. But is it possible for the reverse to be true?

1. THE UNDER-GROUND HOUSE

The aerial image of underground houses from *Architecture without Architects*, reproduced in John Lin's introduction (p. 6), comes from a collection of photographs taken by the German pilot Wulf Dieter Graf zu Castell between 1933-1936. The photo is difficult to discern at first. Barren trees provide a clue of orientation and scale. Looking closer, it is possible to identify people as well: small figures alone and in groups, their shadows cast long against the flat earth. Scattered between the darkened pits are mounds and faint paths traced into the ground. Rudofsky's text identifies these different elements as a village in northern China, outside of Xi'an in Shaanxi province, where life is lived in underground houses.

The assembled figures are undoubtedly looking upwards, perhaps witnessing an aircraft for the first time. In *China-flug* (1938), a publication of Graf zu Castell's photos, two other images accompany the selected by Rudofsky. They are of the landscape that surrounds the underground houses: a terrain of porous loess soil comprising sand swept southward from the Gobi Desert, flat and marked with precise, narrow plots of land. This pattern of agricultural productivity is interrupted by gaping canyons where the edge of the farmland crumbles into a void below, revealing the fragility of the soil and the erosive processes of time. In the center of these photos, a cluster of underground houses and trees are dwarfed by the extension of the flatlands and the scale of the crumbling canyons.

Underground houses are cut into this soil. Some are carved into cliff-sides while others are dug directly into the ground. They begin as uneven pits, but as farmers work to remove the earth they slowly grow, becoming cubic voids twice as wide as they are deep. This void becomes a courtyard for rooms of roughly equal dimensions that are cut, one by one, into its walls, penetrating perpendicularly eight to ten meters into the earth. For centuries, the methods and tools for digging these underground houses were the same—soft earth was scraped and shoveled with rudimentary instruments and carried away in make-shift buckets. The underground house is accessed by a ramp that begins some distance from the main pit, sloping downwards into the ground and then cutting over to open through a decorated threshold into the courtyard. These dwellings share the same organizational structure as the Chinese courtyard house, where communal life takes place in an open, introverted space that distributes individual activities into rooms of their own.

The landscape of the underground house has historically been one of intense poverty. Centuries-old patterns of deforestation and farming have led to the degradation of an already inhospitable soil. Earthquakes render the loess into a liquid slush during the trembling and have wiped out entire villages. The region was also known for its isolation and banditry, leaving residents with few resources to make lives for themselves—perhaps leading to the radical frugality of the houses. Aided by their neighbors or working alone, farmers undertook this slow process of excavation when they finished laboring in the fields. This process could take several years to complete. More than most types of architecture, the underground house needs regular care to keep the loess soil from eroding; water and a layer of lime and plaster are applied at regular intervals. Without this attention, without inhabitation, the walls of the courtyard eventually crumble into themselves and the cubic void becomes a pit again in a process that reverses its creation.

The government's ambitions for the region include the development of paved roads that link the villages to the larger infrastructure networks connecting all of China. To make this possible, the fragile, upper layers of soil are cut away to reach more solid ground below; radical grade changes and new localized topographies now mark the roadside. Houses that had been below ground sometimes have rooms that open onto newly completed streets. With this development, residents have been able to move away from subsistence farming to grow fruit and other cash crops that are transported to market towns. But this has meant that children can now also study in those towns, or attend university in cities, eventually establishing lives outside of the village, as is the case all over rural China.

Older couples remain in villages supported by remittances, taking care of the household as well as young grandchildren. When their grown-up children return home, they are pulled by the obligation to maintain their ancestral homestead. Encouraged by government schemes to engage in heritage activities and tourism, they transform their underground houses into hotels and restaurants for guests. Some villages have reconceived the individual underground dwellings, linking one courtyard to another with new tunnels, and introducing new programs into each space: tourists can shop, eat, and sleep as they make their way from courtyard to courtyard, never breaking the surface of the ground. But these possibilities and the government's promise to support renovations with aid come with long term challenges. Transformations need to be sustained.

These activities have also introduced changes within underground houses. Toilets and showers are now commonplace and are often ventilated, resolving problems with humidity. Traditional *kang* beds—wide brick or earthen platforms that are heated from the channeled air exhausted from nearby stoves—have been replaced by mattresses and white sheets. The courtyard offers an isolated space entirely cut-off from even the village around it. For tourists, the underground house offers a *simulacra* of country life.

Families have also adapted their houses with new additions above ground. These small constructions, sometimes made with the help of local builders, are modest narrow structures a single room deep along their length. They lie within the perimeter of the household's land, sometimes adjacent to the courtyard entrance ramp. Fences are also now commonplace, demarcating the perimeter and securing the households. Families move from above to below ground, depending on the season or the weather. The heat of the summer makes the darkened courtyard rooms more comfortable. In the winter the earth radiates its stored energy, warming the house. Cooking may take place all year in the courtyard. Above ground, the new additions have other conveniences: toilets, a constant flow of air, and heating that is easy to regulate. But the rules are not fixed; the spaces above and below are linked together in one idea of dwelling, the earth's datum a new threshold within that singular realm.

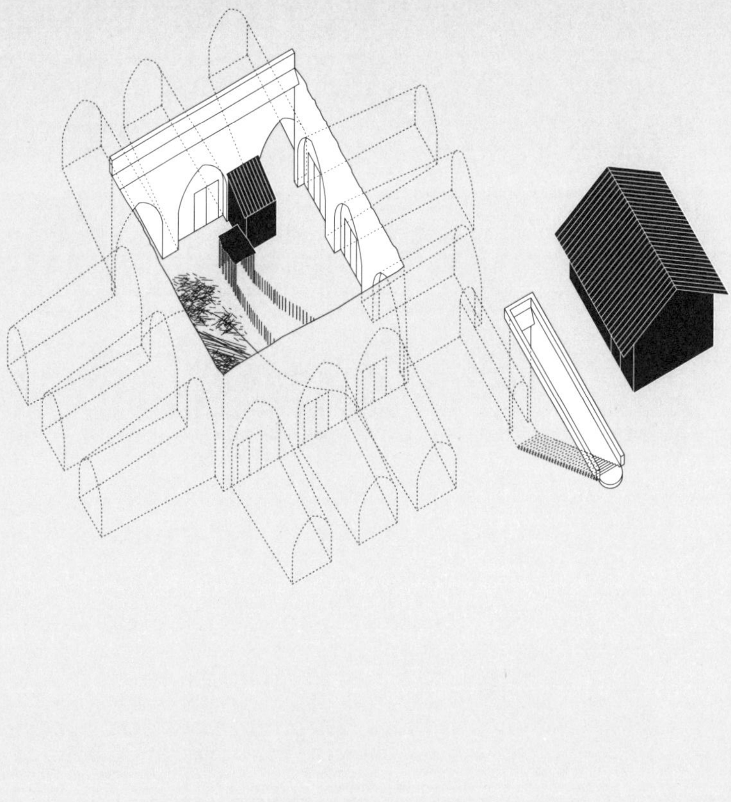

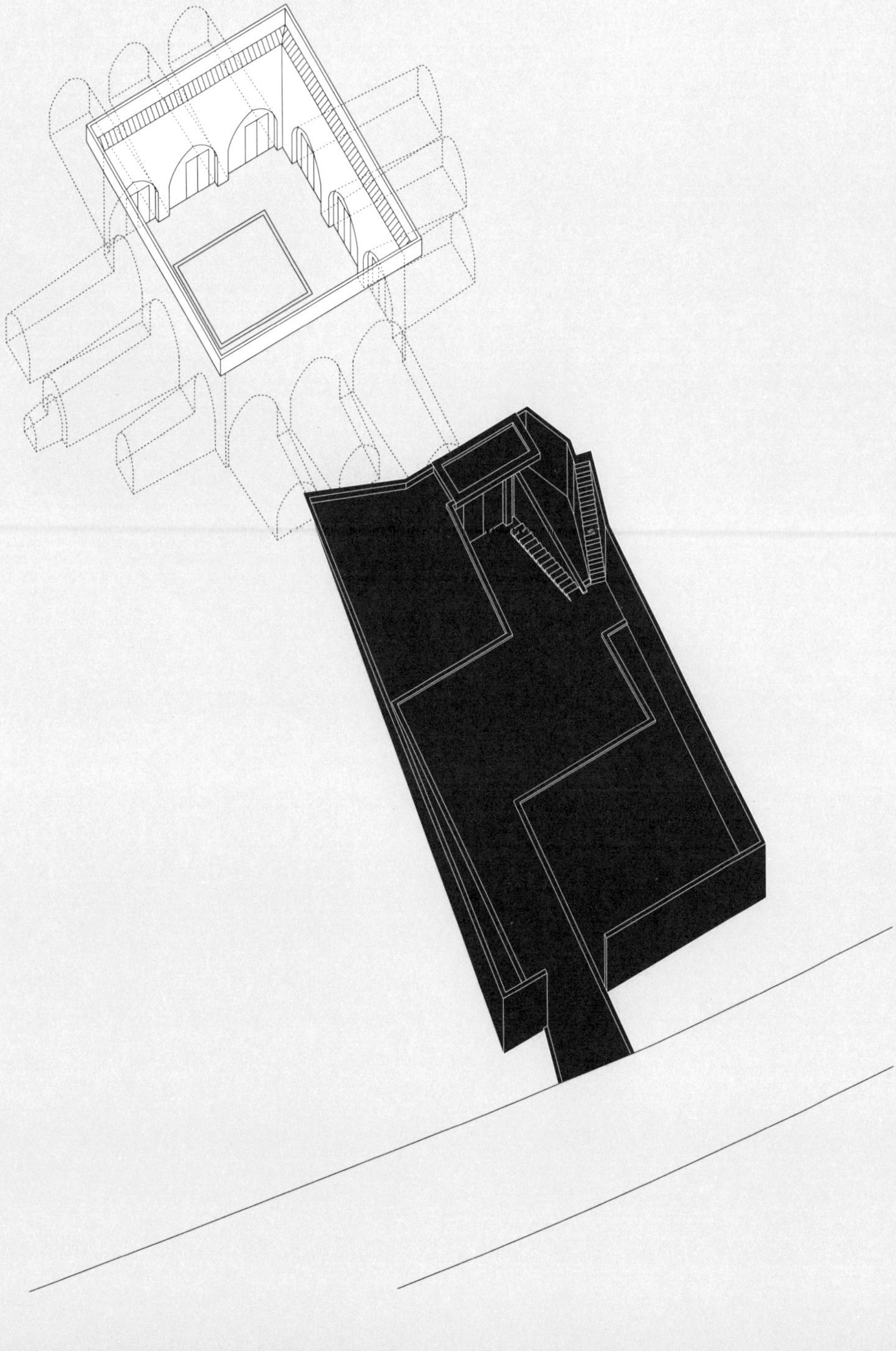

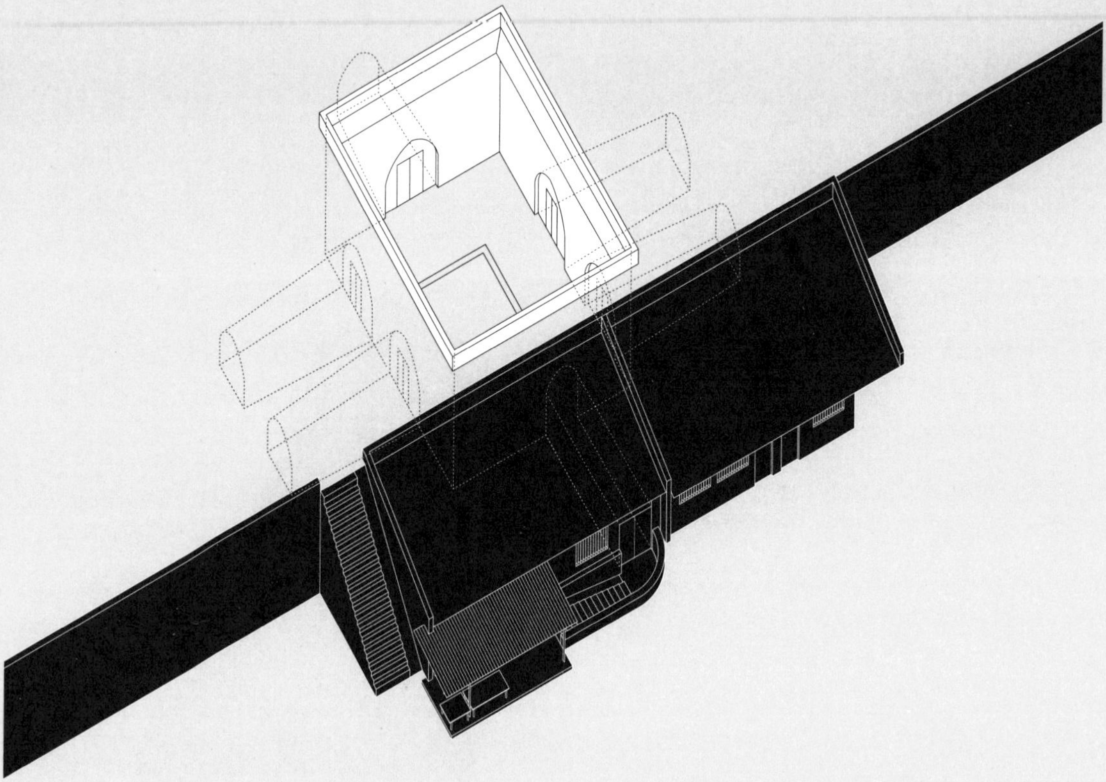

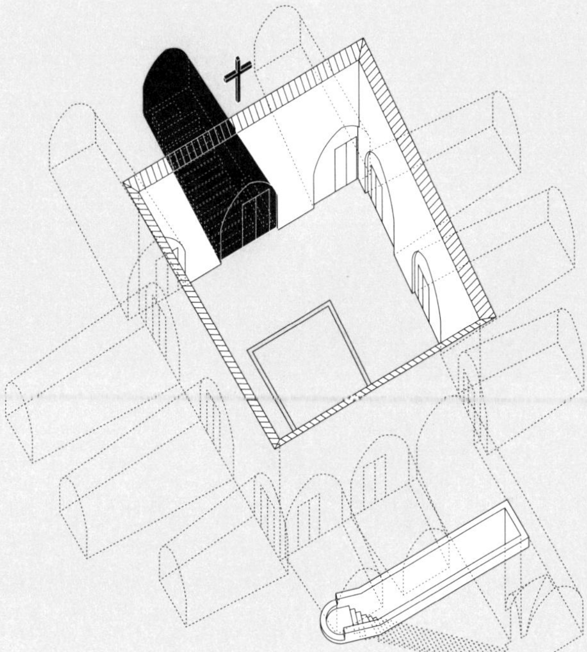

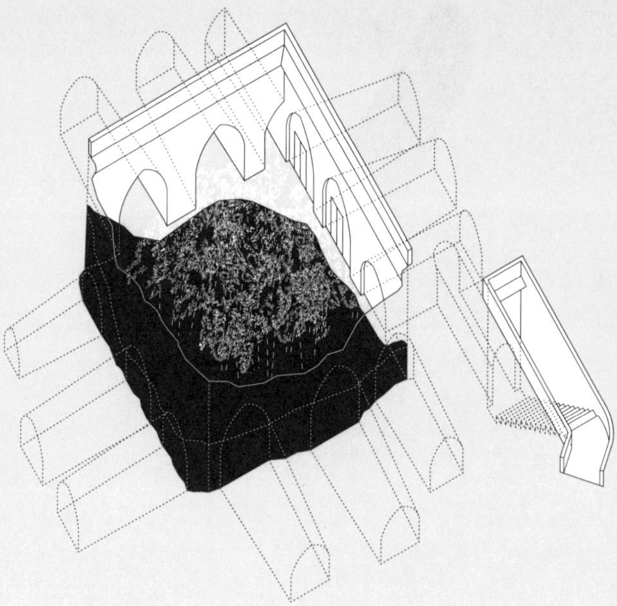

高家地坑院
停车

SUMMER WINTER HOUSE

The family did not abandon their underground house when they built a new house above. Instead, they continue to live underground in the summer and winter, when the climate is extreme. In the summer, the mass of the ground keeps the rooms at a comfortable temperature; the depth of the sunken courtyard prevents the intense rays of the sun from reaching its floor. In the winter, when temperatures drop below freezing and strong winds scrape the flat, sparse landscape, the earth radiates collected heat and offers protection from the strong gusts. Even in the fall and spring months, when the underground rooms become humid and uncomfortable, not all activities take place in the house above and the family continues to cook in the courtyard. To make this back and forth from above to below ground possible, they positioned the new house next to the ramp that cuts into the earth and leads to the courtyard. From summer to winter, or in the daily cycle, this movement from underground to above becomes a new way of inhabiting the time of dwelling and the depth of the ground.

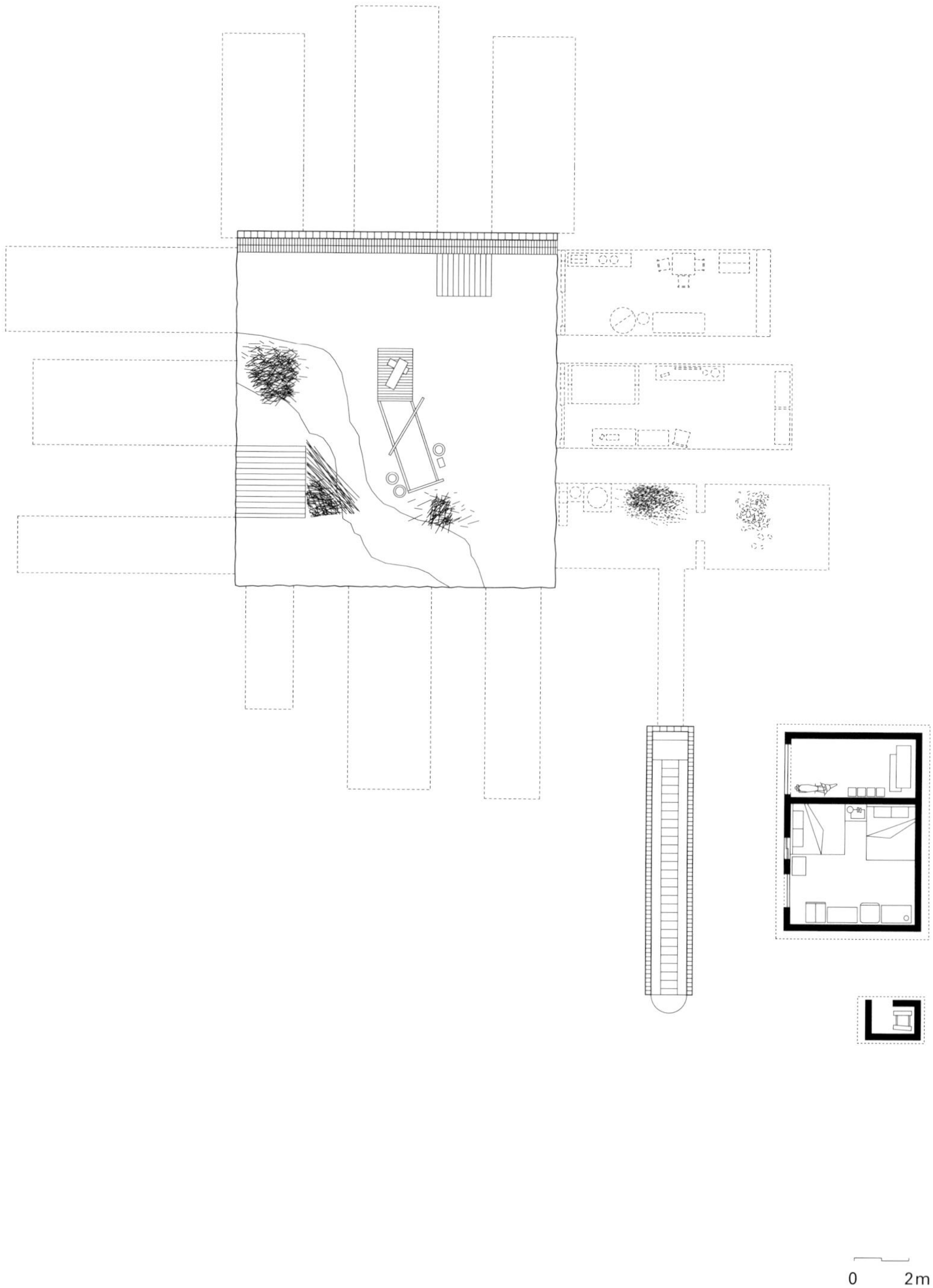
0
2m

DS150
VS125

DRIVE-IN HOUSE

When the eldest son returned from the city to take over his parents' home, he applied for a government subsidy to transform their underground house into a restaurant for tourists. He started by building a new entrance to the sunken courtyard: a ramp large enough for a car to drive straight in. Between the ramp and a newly paved street he built a parking area for visiting guests and a landscaped garden with shaded seating. Red lanterns mark the entrance to the parking area and also hang above the sunken courtyard, creating a ceiling of floating lights. In one corner of the courtyard are a pile of logs that fuel the traditional stoves. Small fruit trees have been planted opposite this cooking area. Some of the dug-out rooms serve as private dining areas, another is a kitchen, and one more a toilet. In the second phase of renovation, the son installed ventilation. The workers pierced narrow holes into the soft earth for pipes that emerge from the flat ground, extracting moisture, smells, and smoke. New uses, modern conveniences, and the technologies that make them possible have transformed the inherited house.

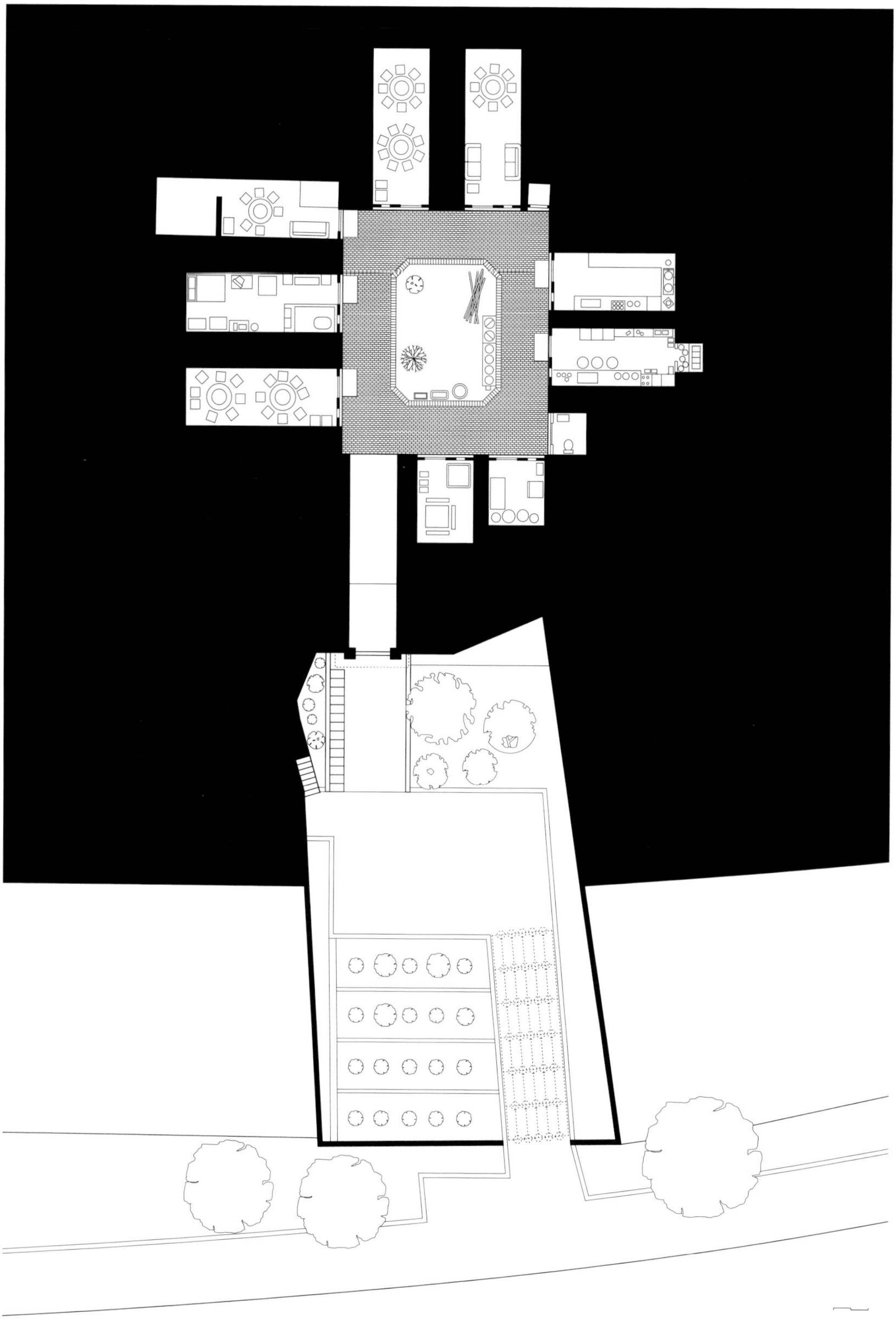

十全十美十大碗

CUT AWAY HOUSE

When the district government built a new road, they cut away earth on one side of this family's house, levelling ground that once enclosed rooms. Neighbors also affected by the construction flattened their plots and replaced their underground houses with generic multistory structures. This family responded differently. Taking advantage of the change of grade created by the excavation, they built a direct entrance into the sunken courtyard from the new street. This entrance comprises a series of rooms—both private rooms and shop-front spaces open to the street. The rooms act as a buffer from the road and as a retaining wall for the original underground construction. An entrance stair parallel to the road descends below grade; then a sharp turn leads to a ramp that descends into the old courtyard. The family supplements their income by selling convenience items and fruit from local orchards to tourists. Rather than raze their underground house, they found a strategy for negotiating a new, abruptly imposed context.

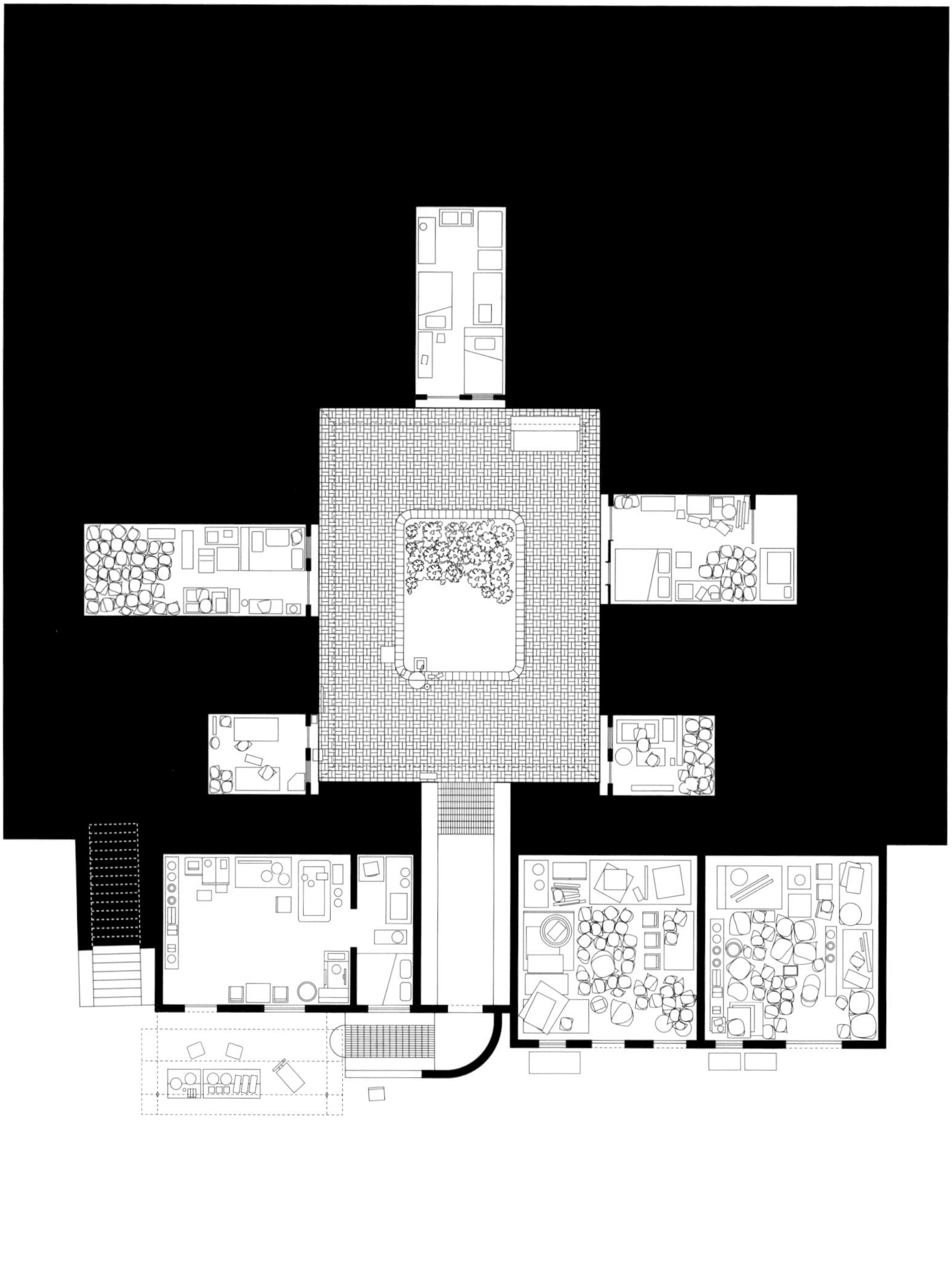
0
2m

市城管局捐赠

CHURCH HOUSE

The dug-out stood empty for almost ten years while the older couple who had built it sought one of their children to take over guardianship. The couple's eldest son and his wife accepted the responsibility, deciding to turn the house into a hotel. With a subsidy from the government and loans from the bank, they repaired and reinforced the dug-out's crumbling earthen vaults with brick, and slowly equipped the rooms to respond to the needs of their new guests. Along with traditional heated *kang* beds that sleep four to five people, they purchased conventional mattresses, tables, and chairs. Recently, they replaced traditional colorful bedding with white linens. They installed toilets in some of the rooms, and drilled holes from the surface for ventilation, eventually adding heating and air-conditioning. One room is arranged with chairs and a central aisle. Until the government asked them to stop and go to the main church in the nearby town, the family conducted Christian services here on Sundays. A cross still hangs above the entrance and is visible from the street. Tourists come from cities and regions all around China as well as other parts of the world, finding the accommodation using reviews on internet sites. When there are no guests, the couple works in their fields—a short walk from the village—where they grow fruit trees and vegetables. The new program for the rooms allows the couple to sustain the dug-out and their own lives.

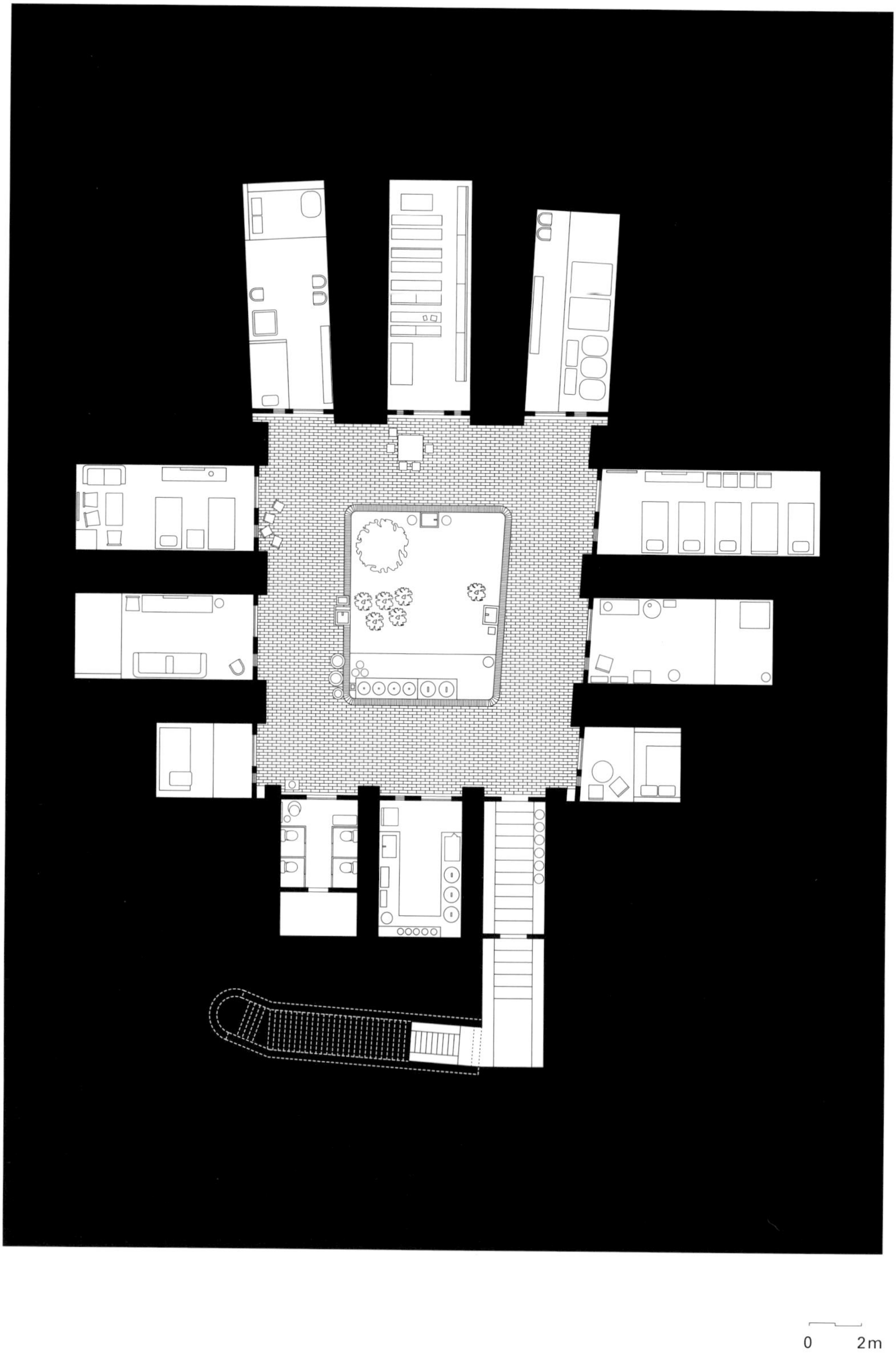
0
2m

以马内利

BACK TO NATURE HOUSE

After some years of neglect, two adjacent sides of the dug-out collapsed inwards. The opposite corner of the courtyard, nevertheless, remained intact, its sharp silhouette defined by a tiled awning. When the family returned to the village to take up the care of their land, they decided to build a new house above ground, using the dug-out courtyard for cooking and its rooms for storage and sleeping when temperatures allowed. To keep the courtyard shaded and cool at midday—even in the summer months—they planted bamboo, vegetables, and a fruit tree on the uneven earth floor. In its half-ruined state, with trees shooting up from the ground, the house seems to have been taken back to nature. Usually, when a dug-out is abandoned the earth falls in on itself. Over time, the pit of the courtyard closes with erosion and sandy soils swept in from the north. For this house, that process was abruptly halted, and the family's daily routine now ensures a renewed productivity. With its earthen ground, garden and bamboo grove, the house inverts the organization of fields above and house below that has characterized life in this region for centuries.

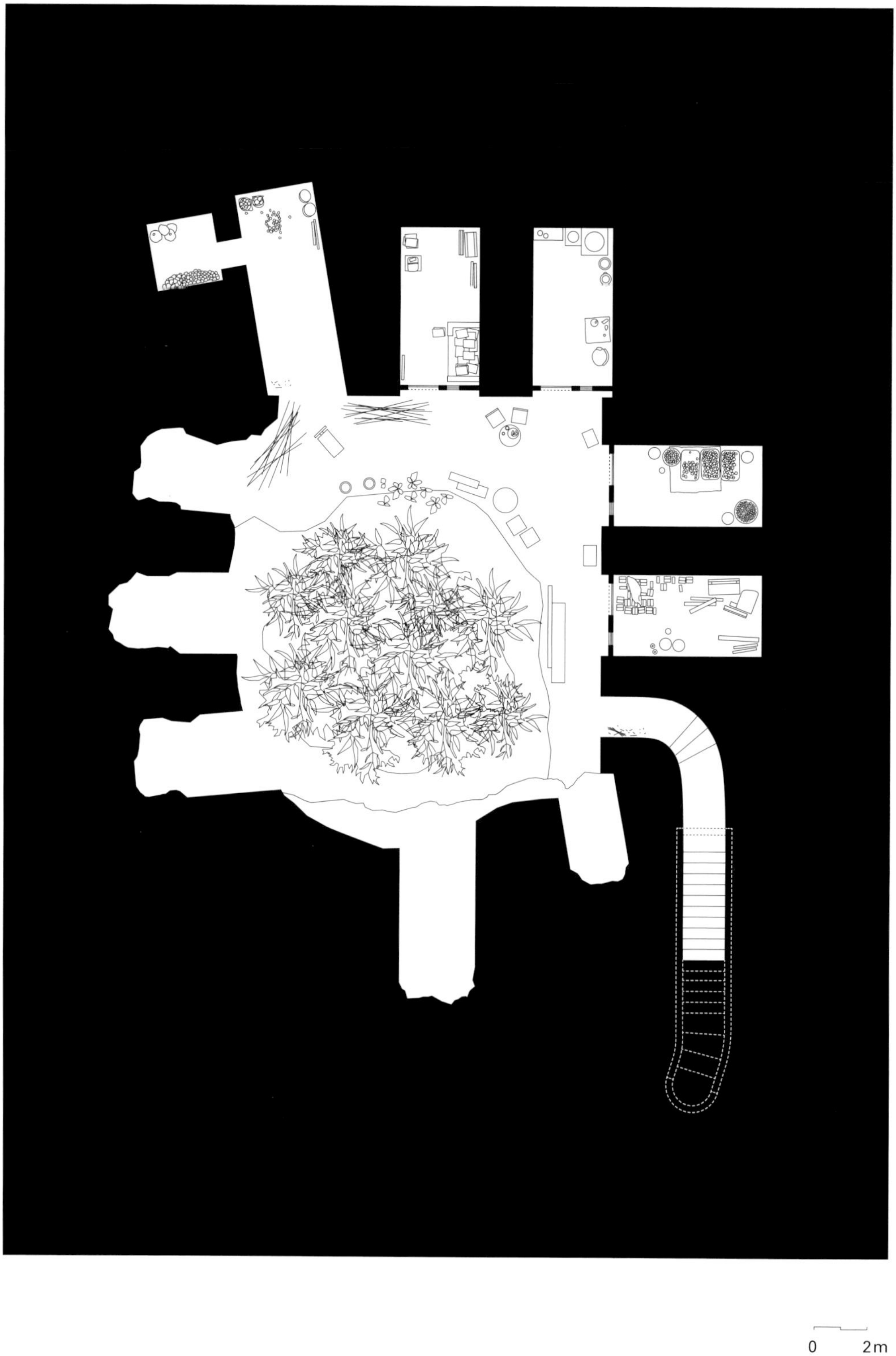
0
2m

The Innkeeper, outside of Xi'an in Shaanxi province, June 2018.

We have been living here for two years, since 2016. Before, for more than two decades, we worked in the city. Then we quit to return home—to return here.

I run this inn with my husband. The accommodation fee from tourists is our main income. We also sell some farm products. We are farmers also. We produce wheat, corn, and fruits on land nearby.

In our village, 115 courtyards have been renovated. Thirty are unrenovated. And 30-40 have already been filled to build modern houses. That was before the government subsidy policy was out. A long time ago the village consisted of only dug-out courtyards: nearly no houses were above ground. In 2014, all the dug-out courtyards were listed as UNESCO World Heritage sites. The government then announced the renovation funding plan for every courtyard: to better protect them.

The dug-outs have gone through many changes. Our ancestors developed this type of housing due to the scarcity of resources. There was no electricity, no roads to the town, etc. The dug-out courtyards solved some basic living problems such as temperature control without electricity. After some years, water wells came to every village with the help of the government. Now some courtyards have running water from the supply above. There are still a few that don't. It depends on the needs that were reported to the government during the 2014 renovations.

Before that, we had to travel to a distant creek to get water. We had a saying that "water is more expensive than oil." Then electricity came. People now have access to air-conditioning and heating systems. The courtyard now is an integration of the old and the new. We find it very pleasant and comfortable to live in.

In June 2016 we opened our dug-out as an inn: two full years now. We are trying our best to accommodate the needs and requests of guests from all over the world. Without damaging the architecture, we increased our space from 13 guests to now welcome 40. Another change was adding bathrooms and showers. We didn't have proper toilets before. We just "dug a hole in the ground and put a bucket in it," as everyone said. The guests couldn't get used to it. So, we began to consider building proper bathrooms.

My husband and I designed the renovations, but we hired people for the construction. We couldn't do it ourselves as it required professional skills. There is heating in every room. The heaters were added later. We are the only family with heaters for hundreds of miles around. Every room here except for the kitchen has heating now. Also, as part of the renovation we added ventilation pipes. The traditional courtyard rooms weren't ventilated properly. We used a *luoyang chan*—a boring tool—to dig a hole from the ground above into the rooms to pass in the pipe. Whenever the door opens, it ventilates. The courtyard rooms aren't like the houses above ground where ventilation is easy. Before the systems were added, people living in the underground rooms tended to develop health problems such as rheumatism. This also affected local eating habits. People here like to eat chili and pepper to get rid of the *shi qi*—body humidity. We added the ventilation system during the second batch of renovations. It was a result of guest complaints. We locals were used to the humidity, but people from other places couldn't handle it.

My husband and I want to further improve this place. Today, we have nine rooms—eight of which are for guests. The bathroom is still shared by everyone. A current plan is to add bathrooms to three or four of the eight rooms, creating a hierarchy for the accommodations: more luxury ones and basic ones. Every room is different. But each has one or two heated beds. The bed is large enough to accommodate three, four, or five people depending on the room. For the three rooms where we would like to add bathrooms, the goal is mainly to turn them into more standard suites. The renovation would cost quite a lot of money, which we cannot spare right now.

The guests come from everywhere —both Chinese and foreigners. We had guests from Switzerland, the United States, and many other places. We know that they are foreign because they look different from us. And we have had Chinese guests from all the provinces. Some of them knew the place from the Internet, some heard from friends, others just somehow found their own way here. On the Internet, we have registered our location on *Gaode*, *Baidu*, and *Sohu*. People can search for our inn. We call ourselves "Gao Family Inn." Of the five inns in the village, we are the only Gao family. So, if you ask, "Where is Gao Family Inn?" people will guide the way for you. Other inns and accommodations have more sophisticated names with deep meanings. We didn't think much on this matter; the name is easy to remember.

Apart from the guests, now it's only my husband, my son, and me. And my son sometimes stays in our house in the town. It is not far: about four kilometers from here. But before, there were many people here: my grandparents, my parents-in-law, my uncles-in-law, my aunt, my aunts-in-law, and their spouses and children. It was a large family, consisting of many small subfamilies. As the family expanded, we gradually ran out of space in the courtyard. Some family members then applied to the government for new housing. As more and more people moved out, the courtyard was left with only my grandparents. There is one characteristic of a *yaodong* that you need to be aware of: when the rooms and the courtyard are occupied daily by the residents, it remains in good condition almost effortlessly. When it is not occupied and left empty, it decays very fast. We started the renovation four years ago with one side of the courtyard already decayed.

The layout and usage of the dug-out remained more or less in its original state. It's only that the material changed from bare mud and soil to the finish with brick and tile. Some people come and say it's not authentic enough, but it was the only choice. To renovate and make the place livable for guests from around the world, we had to introduce some contemporary elements to the traditional. Now our courtyard is both old and new. Some guests once wanted to experience the most authentic *yaodong*, so I took them to the unrenovated rooms. They changed their minds as soon as they walked in. It is too dark inside.

Twenty years ago, my husband and I worked in the town. We weren't very rich, but we had a stable salary to support ourselves. We worked in a synthetic fiber factory, producing some semi-finished products. My husband quit in 2008 and I quit in 2010. We were both very tired of factory life. He then became a long-distance driver. I stayed at home and tried to look for some part-time jobs. We spent a few years without having a settled job, just wandering around mostly. We finally came back to the village in 2016, mainly because my husband's parents were getting old and needed some care from us. My husband's younger brother and his wife moved from the village to town in 2014. It was almost like we switched our lives around. When we came back, we tried to farm at first. We weren't very good at it. We needed to learn from the more experienced.

My husband and I had to take over the courtyard, and also, of course, the financial responsibility. Even with the subsidy, it would still cost us over 200,000 yuan. In the villages, our income mainly depends on the fruit trees. The annual income was around 10,000 yuan, at most. We had to purchase tools, farming supplies, pay for the workers. We knew that taking over the courtyard meant taking over a great debt, but we still had to do it, since we are the eldest of the siblings. We made a written promise to my parents-in-law that we will clear our debts in three years.

When we first started, there was nothing: no Wi-Fi, no toilets, no heater. Nothing. We used to have traditional duvet covers with colorful patterns. Then we realized, even though we washed them for every new guest, that they didn't like them because they couldn't tell by their eyes if they were clean or not. When we did the renovation later, I changed all of them to white linens. The set up gradually transformed from a more rural style to a more widely acceptable one. The renovation plan is constantly being adapted to customers' feedback.

We want not only to earn money, but also to live our lives and make friends. We don't like to put excessive effort on advertising. We want everything to be spontaneous. When there are no guests, we do some farming. We want to keep the farmland so that when people step into our courtyard, they know they are in an authentic farmer's family. We also let our guests go pick ingredients from our land and cook themselves. Our only request is not to waste any food.

We have some financial needs, inevitably. We have elderly family members to look after and younger ones to prepare for their wedding. On top of all this, we still have some debts. In the future, if financially possible, we would like to travel around ourselves, to see what other places are like. They must be very different from here.

But I love the village. We have over 400 families. It seems like a large population, but in fact it is not. Most of the residents now are older, over 50 years old. People younger than 40 mostly left for the town or cities. All the villagers are very friendly to each other. It is quite the opposite from how people get along in the city. We have experienced both.

When I lived in the city, my day to day was always the same. From home to factory, from factory to home. Same routine every day. The only place we went outside of work was to the market to get food for cooking. We didn't have the chance to make friends. But it's all different now. In our courtyard, we have control over what we do every day. On summer nights, women my age go down to the central square for some dancing after dinner. Other people just sit on the side and chat with each other. The village doesn't have a lot of cultural facilities like the city, but that doesn't matter. We feel perfectly content when we simply sit outside and enjoy the breeze. When we were in the town, I got mad at every little thing that went wrong. Nowadays, I don't get mad at anything.

Living in the Summer Winter House, outside of Sanmenxia, Henan province, September 2018.

The courtyard is several decades old—at least 30 years—and the house was built almost 20 years ago. Then people started to not want to go down into the courtyard. That is when we built the house above. We built it for convenience. We hired some workers to help us. It wasn't expensive. The labor was cheap. It was about 10 yuan per person per day. Now it is at least 100 yuan. The construction did not take so long: a few days, I think. The bricks too were not so expensive. Around here it used to be all mud houses, but now we are using bricks.

Before it was all flat land and we dug out the courtyard with workers we hired. We used hand-tools. The soil and sand was carried away in a basket. During the 1980s, excavation machinery came in. If our courtyards decay, we can ask workers to come in and fix them. If there is no decay or damage, you just leave them. But nowadays it is impossible to build new ones. The workers who used to make them are all elderly or have passed away. In some of the courtyards, there have been four or five generations.

The land before was all flat and the road was a dirt trail before they turned it into pavement. The old trail was inconvenient. When it rained it was hard for the cars to get through. We live up here in the house in colder days and move down when it gets hot. In hotter days, we go down to the courtyard after meals for some rest. But mostly we live in the house up here because it is a lot more convenient. We eat in the house. The kitchen is also here. We don't go to the courtyard for eating. Now we use it to store things. There is another family who built a small shed in their underground courtyard. It is not as good as my shed.

My eldest child is already 36 years old. I am already 55 years old. My husband is 60 years old. We have been living here since her birth: before that was when we dug the courtyard. Yes, at least 40 years ago.

And before this, we lived in another courtyard which is over 100 years old. We were still at the old courtyard when we got married. There were three of us: my husband, his father, and me. But he passed away some time ago—my husband's father—and the old courtyard has been renovated by the second brother. My husband has two older brothers. And a few sisters. He's the third eldest son in the family. So, it was the second oldest brother who took over the old courtyard. It is a lot better than this courtyard of mine! But it is locked up.

My two daughters got married and went off to live in their husbands' houses. My daughter-in-law and my son moved to Sanmenxia together. And a small grandson also lives in the city. Back in the days there was a school near here. Then after some years the students had all moved to the city. The students used to come here after their classes. Now, the nearest school is some distance away. Even that school does not have many students. Only my husband and I live here now. Last time, I think you saw my younger daughter. She doesn't live here anymore; she lives down the road with her husband. During the festival times, usually the family can't get together. The younger ones can't always get off from work. Or they come back here a little late: usually the second day of the lunar new year.

II.

THE WOODEN HOUSE

The wooden houses of the Dong people occupy river valleys that thread through three provinces in south-central China. The relationships between place, cultural identity, and craft that defined their traditional wooden architecture have been radically altered by new construction processes that make use of inexpensive industrial materials and require little skill. In other parts of China, similar changes have led to the replacement of traditional village fabric with generic concrete-frame structures, completed with brick or block infill and tile cladding. In Dong villages, such generic constructions are increasingly found alongside collisions between old and new building methods that result in innovative tectonic solutions and spatial prototypes that afford new ways of living.

The Dong did not adopt a written script until the 20th century, and relied on oral transmission, material artifacts, and ritual to tell the stories of their history. The wooden houses represent an important part of this identity, comprising an aspect of material culture whose fabrication and character are laden with significances. This makes any transformation all the more important for how the community sees itself. The builders within this region aim to maintain the cultural specificity of their community while recognizing that social and economic shifts have changed people's lives. The act of building becomes a way of negotiating these competing forces.

The traditional relationship between building and Dong identity is crystallized in the wooden frame structure that provides the underlying spatial organization for the home. The houses were traditionally built with China fir harvested from surrounding villages. Specific rituals accompany the felling of trees, the marking and cutting of logs into sized members and joints, and the day-long assembly of the components into a completed frame. This final act often brings together the entire village and needs to be completed in a single day that is carefully chosen in advance.

The hand-ink master, responsible for calculating the lengths of each member and the angles of joints, occupies a respected and often hereditary place within the village. While many men help with carpentry—preparing wood, assembling the prepared pieces—few attain the status of hand-ink master. This process largely takes place without drawings and almost entirely as a function of the hand-ink master's accumulated knowledge and intuitive building sense. Know-how is developed and shared through the very practice of building. The frame acts as a scaffold for the work that follows.

Floors, walls, windows, and furniture were traditionally crafted of the same China fir as the house itself. This wood was also used for boats—once common on the rivers that link valley villages—and for coffins stored in the spaces below elevated houses. While the frame is assembled and raised in one auspicious day, the rest of the house can be completed when time, labor, and money allow. Every village will have one or two completed frames at some point during the year, with the top-most, golden beam often still decorated with a red ribbon. Ceremonies are meant to ensure both the safety of the workers as they climb the heights of the structure and the prosperity of those who will live in the completed house.

The open nature of the frame, defined by several equivalent bays, welcomes improvisation. First-floor rooms are organized around an open central area where a fire is sometimes kept. Sleeping, resting, or the storage of goods can take place in any of the rooms. The second floor is often partly unenclosed, open to the wind.

In villages today, the possibility of building to fulfill contingent needs and alter houses over time has introduced new methods of construction, inscribing changing programmatic needs into the armature of the Dong frame. Villagers are attached to the cultural value of their wooden homes and modestly proud of the more recent attention their ways of living have received from tourists arriving on road and high-speed rail connections. Yet, they also recognize the fragility of traditional ways of building.

As the piles of Dong houses are not founded into the earth but instead rest on stacked stones, ever more unpredictable floods can sweep away entire structures. Because older dwellings were constructed with mortise and tenon joints that locked into place, these houses would float like rafts along the torrent until they impacted an obstacle and shattered. Other times, the earth of collapsed hillsides would flow into streams of mud, filling ground floors where household items, tools, and appliances are stored. The wooden houses are also difficult to heat, wire, and equip with plumbing.

With villagers returning from the city, or with remittances needing to be invested, money goes to adaptations and adjustments that address these risks. Local regulations allow for certain changes to be made, particularly to ground floors where concrete and brick constructions replace or interlace with the wooden piles. Where before the ground floor was left unenclosed to negotiate the terrain, today it is often leveled and enclosed by plastered brick walls, creating spaces for kitchens and toilets.

Villages along valley roads have seen the greatest changes. Concrete requires industrial materials to be shipped from nearby towns and calls for a new set of skills. Village carpenters embrace these ways of building, integrating them into knowledge they have carried forward from the past. The sons or daughters of carpenters are likely to study in a nearby city and return with a degree in engineering, architecture, or forestry management. If they return to the village and take up their father's practice, they work with newly available materials, using CAD drawings or models for reference during construction.

While the cost of building a concrete house is more or less equivalent to that of a wood construction, concrete moves along more quickly and requires relatively less skill to accomplish. Unlike a wooden house, the shell of a concrete house provides an enclosed space that can be occupied almost immediately. The spatial finiteness of concrete offers a different kind of affordance than the equal bays of the wooden frame. Some concrete constructions incorporate balconies or entire floors in wood. These hybrid structures are sometimes made from the disassembled frame of an unused house in a neighboring village or valley. Each transported element is numbered in chalk to indicate its place within the renewed structure.

The wooden house resulted in a fabric of shared life within Dong villages that linked exterior spaces to a more private life within. The close proximity of houses, adjacent constructions connected at their upper story by walkways, and terraces that extended domestic life, meant that the houses were part of a larger network of spatial relations that reflected the complexity of village family bonds. The new hybrid constructions reflect a changed relationship to these family structures, with the links binding an entire village becoming less important than the immediate extended family. With their more inward orientation, the hybrid constructions sometimes do not address the world outside in a way that participates in the vital, collective affordance that characterized traditional Dong house. As villages are transformed by new constructions, self-builders may also look to reassert this communal dimension with hybrid tectonic experiments that address changed ways of living together within Dong communities.

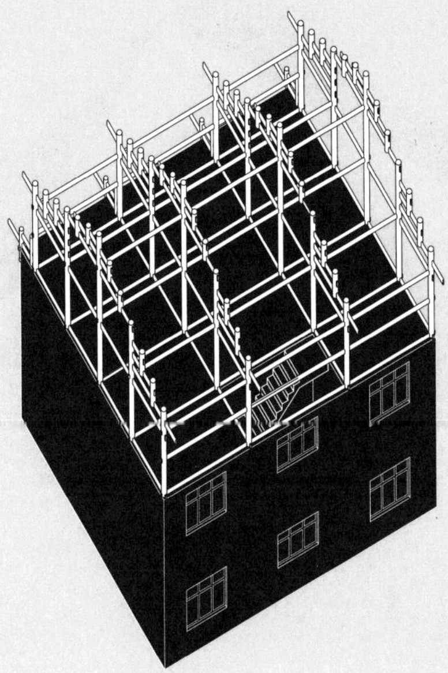

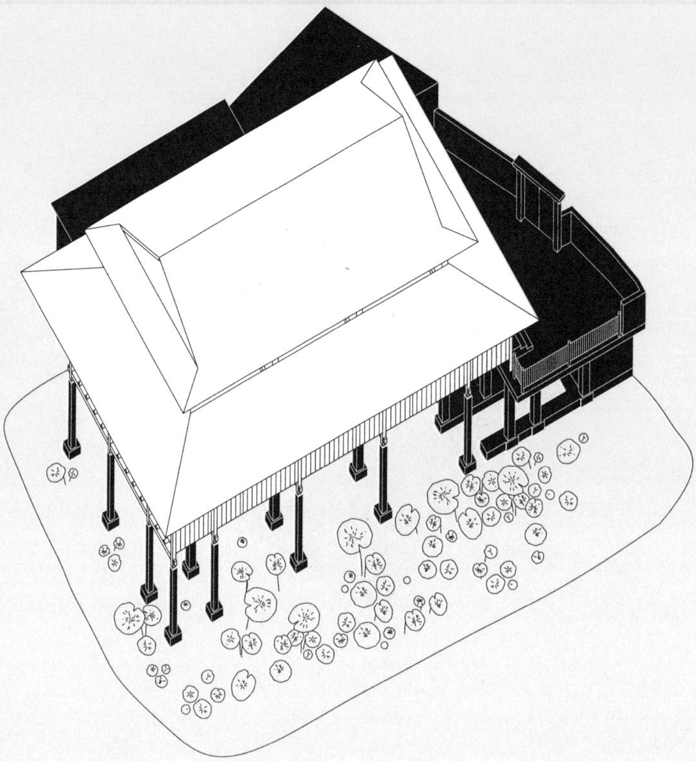

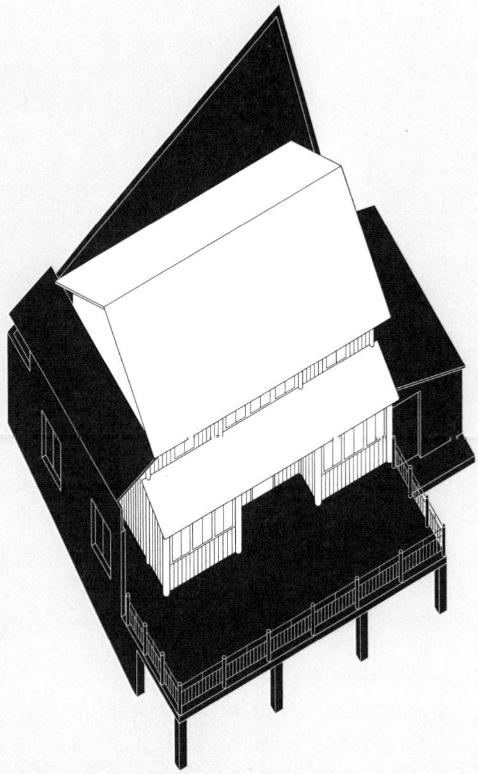

時來萬事和

HIGHWAY HOUSE

The original house was dismantled and reassembled next to a new highway that runs along a river winding through the valley. The house sits on a new concrete structure, comprising a frame raised from the banks by columns and connected to the road with a footbridge. The highway house now serves as a government checkpoint for trucks delivering goods to the valley. In its earlier configuration, wooden piles would have extended from the ground into the house. Because these piles often rested only on stacked stone foundations, houses would sometimes be swept away by frequent floods. Today, the concrete elements are separate from the wooden structure, and the house is protected from the water below. The process of taking apart and reassembling the house in its new site is made visible by the numbered wooden columns, panels, and frames. With the concrete adaptation, it was possible to reuse the elements of the house in a new situation.

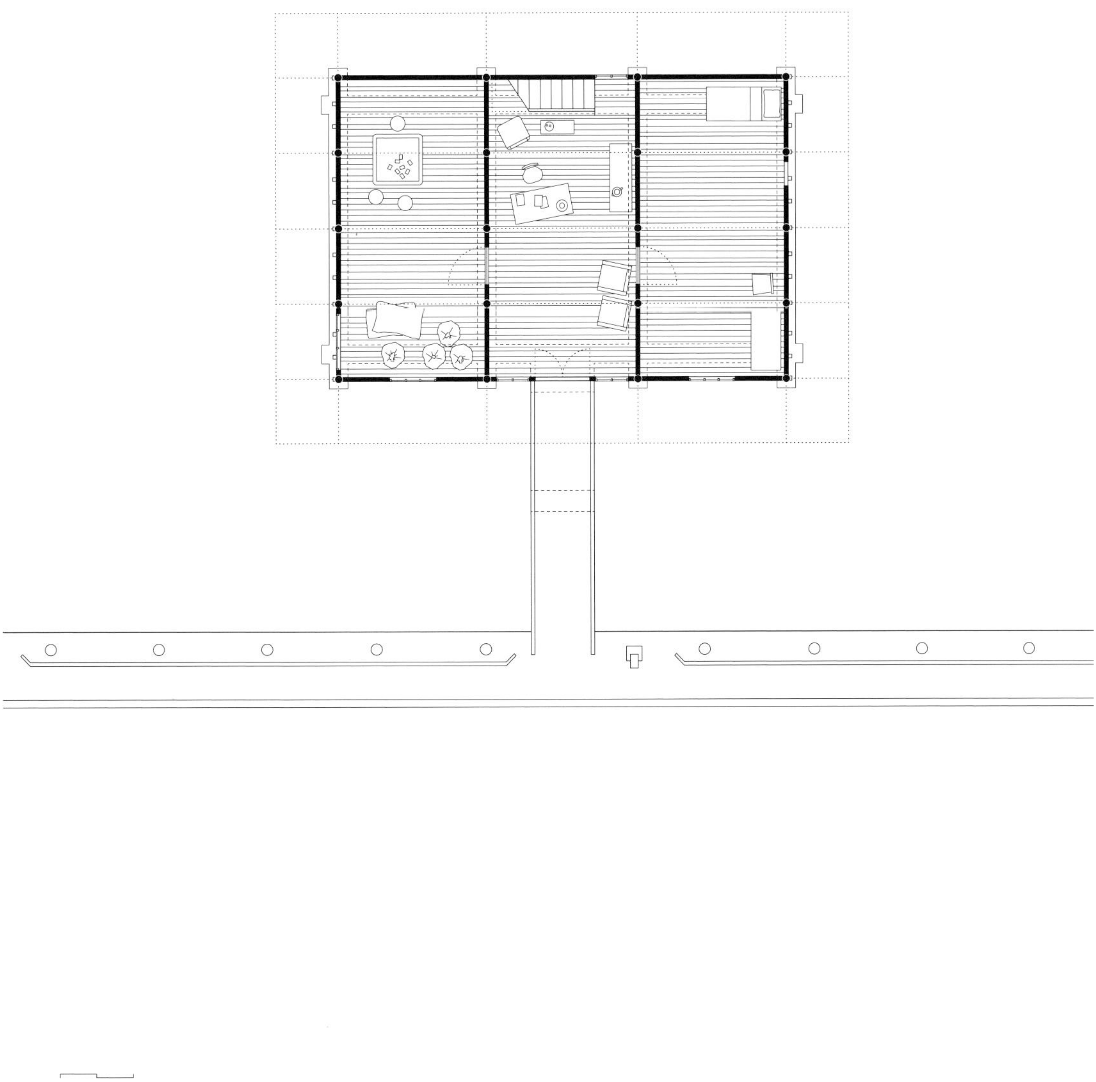
0
2 m

HOUSE ON HOUSE

The family decided to add a wooden frame and pitched roof on top of their concrete house. The dimensions and spatial organization of both houses follow a traditional spatial diagram: three even bays with an open middle area flanked by four equal rooms. In traditional houses this meant that the main space would often be used for a fire; other rooms had no fixed use and could be adapted to a family's needs. Above the main door of the concrete house is a recessed balcony that looks onto the fields. Openings in the facade are filled with aluminum windows. The brick infill has mostly been plastered and painted white. A stair at the back leads to a second level, crowned by the traditional frame of a wooden house, that has been left unenclosed. This is often the case in traditional houses; the family smokes meats, dries crops, and stores handicrafts in this open space. The void formed by the pitched roof almost doubles the height of the top floor. The everyday activity of the family shifts between the generic concrete construction below and the traditional open structure above. The house stitches together old and new, taking what is useful from both.

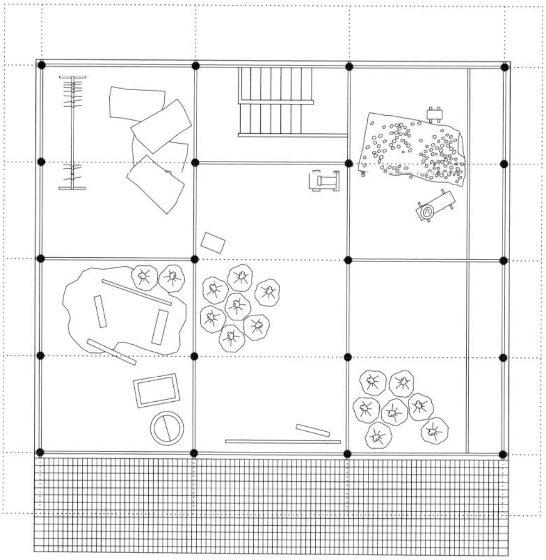

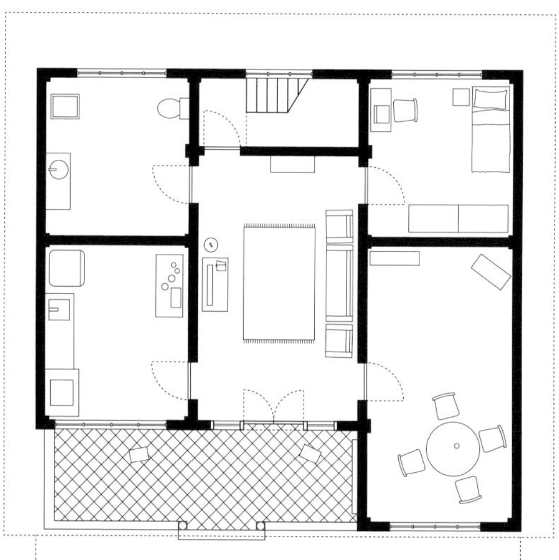

0 2m

强力斗车
P FEED

POND HOUSE

The house once occupied a remote hillside overlooking a village that sloped into a valley. The owners wanted to be closer to a new road that would connect them to nearby towns, so they disassembled the wooden elements of their home and numbered each one, transporting the pieces to a new site once the road was completed. The location for the reassembled house posed new challenges: steps away was a river that flooded during the rainy season, which meant permanent exposure to moisture. The wooden stilts that before raised the house were cut down to stumps. The house now rests on tall brick columns, each sitting on a concrete base founded into the ground of a marshy pond. In the gap between the street level and the raised ground floor is a concrete terrace with neat piles of firewood and leftover construction material. After building the terrace, the family added a concrete volume with a kitchen to the rear of the house; underneath, almost surrounded by the water, they completed a small brick volume for a toilet. Noise, dust, and exhaust from the main road soon became difficult to live with, so they added an enclosed wooden porch raised from the pond on thin concrete columns. The family now pass through this intermediate space to enter the original wooden structure. A new terrace on the house's shorter side leads to the street. Gates were then added for safety. The in-between spaces resulting from the challenges of the new site added new and unexpected qualities —mediating between the house, the water, and the road.

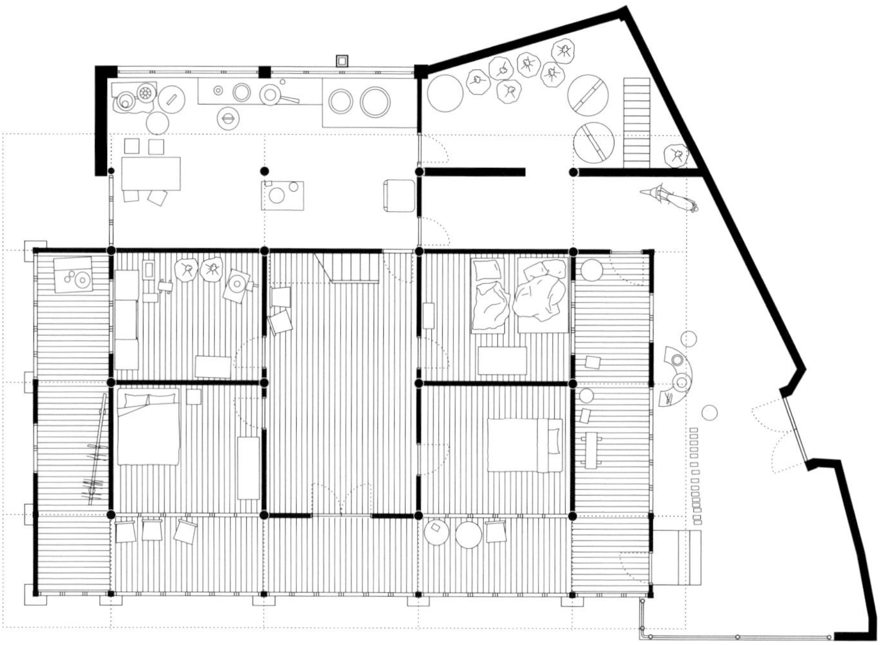

0
2 m

液化

WALL HOUSE

The traditional wooden house fully occupies its irregular site with new concrete frame elements. The main road fronting the house winds through the valley and connects villages to the district town. Between the road and the traditional wooden house, the family built a platform raised from the ground on concrete columns. Underneath, they store building equipment, tools, and a scooter. At the rear of the site is a new addition whose triangular plan extends nearly to the plot line. The bare concrete frame structure, which has mostly been left unfinished, does not impose itself on the wooden house. The development of these additions has been slow and incremental, with the family relying on installments of money sent back by their two sons. Along the back wall of the house, beneath a large triple window, they have installed a countertop with a sink and space for cooking. In the narrowest corner of the triangular room, a tightly compressed space leads to the most recent addition. For many months, there was simply a brick wall parallel to the side of the house. When funds became available, they covered the space with a pitched roof, creating an enclosed passageway from the front platform to the back. On the opposite side, there is a similar-sized space that is used as a toilet. In the future, perhaps the front platform will also be enclosed, creating a circuit of spaces with the wooden house at the center.

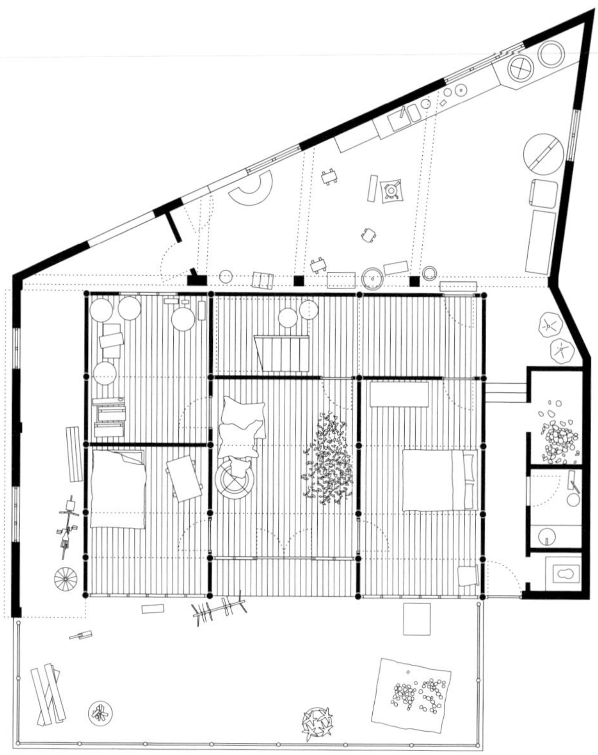

0
2m

SHELL HOUSE

After the residents assembled and raised the house's wooden frame and completed the roof, they used concrete and brick to build an exterior shell. Brick walls could be completed faster and required less skill than the traditional method of joining wooden elements to create an infill. Where traditionally joined wooden enclosures allow drafts of air and sound from the street, the new shell is nearly impervious to wind and noise. The shell comprises a thin wall that rises two-stories and is set off from the structural wooden grid (in most cases by a few centimeters). Inside the house, wooden partitions that enclose a small area contrast with smooth, finished surfaces elsewhere. Pipes for a kitchen and bathroom are fixed to the plastered wall. On the short end of the house, wooden stairs have been slipped between the wooden frame and the shell. Plastering stops on the second floor; from there upwards, the rough bricks are left unfinished, climbing the entire height of the gable end. In the juncture between the stacked bricks and the roof structure, an inversed "V" of light illuminates the gap. One manner of living is embedded within another in the meeting of bare plastered walls and wood.

打 月租免费V网免费

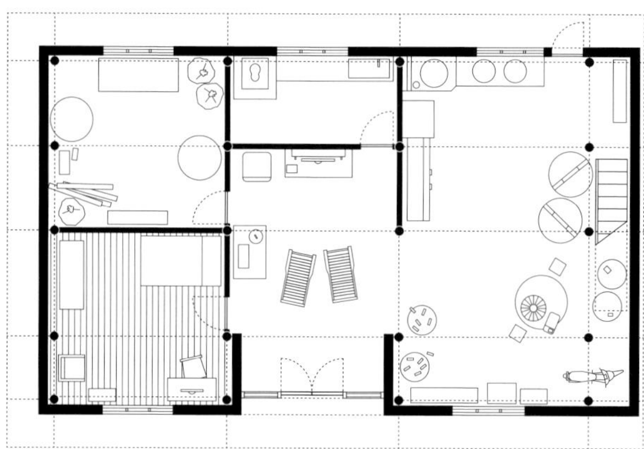

0
2 m

貴客賀喜心添喜
富貴永恒
Eternal wealth
芒果汁

地久天長
志趣相投地久天長

万 和

The Carpenter's Son, in Liping county, Guizhou province, July 2018.

I started learning carpentry in 2011. My father started in 1982. I started after university where I studied computer science and software engineering. Now, I don't use that so much except that I draw on the computer: mostly with AutoCAD but also now I am learning Sketchup.

Today, there are fewer young people working on carpentry. But I returned because of my family. My father and my father's three older brothers are all carpenters. They learned from their uncle on their mother's side. He was also a carpenter, but he passed away. Most carpenters in this area learned from him. My father has been working as a carpenter for 30 years. He finished junior high school and then he was in the army in Yunnan for about two years.

When I was really young, I always watched my granduncle teaching my father and his brothers. If they had questions, they would go to him. And then my father became a hand-ink master. I think it took him about five years, although some people work their entire life as carpenters and still are unable to do the work of the hand-ink master. You have to be able to absorb the details: to pay attention and not forget. Some carpenters, even though they might know the overall scheme of the building, will not understand the details: measurement is important and being able to calculate.

The hand-ink master will draw the structure and then sometimes make small models. Today some do everything on the computer. But I still make models. The older hand-ink masters didn't need to think so much about structure; they already know, without reflecting on it. I learned fast because I was learning at the same time that I was practicing. Sometimes there are building problems, and I figured out quickly how to deal with them. And then I learned how to consider these problems in advance when working on the drawings.

For houses, we still build in wood but also with a mix of concrete and brick. I still haven't made drawings of such a project: only for the wooden houses. For hybrid houses, I usually only draw the wooden part on the top. For the more complex projects, if I don't draw the wooden part first, there will be mistakes. These days we have very few house projects. Houses are too complicated. Of course, the structures themselves are simple. Many people know how to do that, and the cost is low. However, it takes a lot of time to install the wooden panels. We need to wait until the panels are dry. If the panels are not dry enough and we install them, they will crack in the future. That is why it is complicated.

Houses that are more than 100 years old have tenon and mortise joints at the center of the columns. These houses are difficult to dismantle. That is why some of the old houses are leaning over but not falling even if the columns are decaying at their base. When you hit the column, the joint will lock. The carpenters today will not build that way because it is difficult to take apart the house or renovate afterwards. But even without such joints, wooden frames are still a bit complicated.

The frame must go very quick because we need to finish in one day—one auspicious day. You need many people to work. The numbers are also based on how many apprentices the hand-ink master can take. It depends how fast he can mark the trunks for the apprentices to work. If there are too many apprentices, the hand-ink master cannot draw as fast as they cut. If he is fast, perhaps five.

Today, the villagers will not usually take part in the work. In the past, say in the '70s and '80s, people still came together to help. And if the family is in poor economic condition, the relatives and friends will come by for the construction work. A contractor can cost several thousand yuan depending on the amount of work—even up to 10,000. The salary for workers is getting more expensive, as is the timber. That is why many people are now building brick houses. The cost of a brick house is lower. For timber houses, the timber structure is not that expensive, but the panels take time and the then it will also take much longer to build.

There are rituals for housebuilding. For example, the raising of the beam. If I build a house for my family, the relatives from the side of the mother-in-law will go to the mountain at four or five in the morning without being noticed by others to steal a tree from our lands. Now this is told to the owner in advance and the tree is bought and waiting. The relatives carry the tree back to the site and it is used for the uppermost beam; often this is a symbolic beam and not structural. The reason is that the golden beam should be a bit curved—not too straight. This means that hopefully, the descendants will not be too straightforward when they say or do things. They need to have some consideration—to leave some space. We also give sweets during the ceremony. Even in new houses we will still do this. Any kind of house. If it is a brick house, usually it has a sloped roof. We will put one wooden beam on the top below the ridge of the house.

Nowadays, whether we conduct the rituals or not does not matter that much. We don't believe in those superstitions any more, but we still do that since some people in the countryside haven't changed those old beliefs. When erecting the frames, there is also a ritual for safety. Nowadays, we have scaffolding with steel frames and other equipment, but the rituals provide an assurance. Other times, there will be a celebration and the whole village will gather to have a meal together. Each person will pay some money for the meal. For example, we built a pavilion recently in the countryside. We began the work in the nighttime. First, we erected a column, and when it was upright there were fireworks.

We have all kinds of houses here. We have an entire timber house, a timber house on top of a brick house, or an entire brick house with a timber frame. The last one costs more. The government does not allow us to build an entire brick house. You need to wrap it with wood. This is the government's requirement. A few years ago, even this kind of house was not allowed by the government. When my father started to build a brick house more than ten people came here from the county government. They said: "Are you going to tear this down by yourself, or do you want us to do it?"

They did not allow us to build with bricks. Then he drew a drawing of a house that was brick in the interior but wood on the exterior. People could not realize this was a brick house from the outside. He showed this drawing to the government people, and they didn't say anything. Then a group of people from the higher county government came to look at his house. They said: "We should promote this style!" They did not allow the lower government to tear it down.

The timber house is not resistant to fire and floods. It is also difficult for installing electricity and sound insulation. The brick house can provide better facilities. When you build in this way, it looks like a timber house from the outside and allows us to preserve the ethnic culture and style. The government wants us to preserve these things, but of course they will not give us any support to help. Even though a wood frame house outside of a brick house costs more money, the government does not have the funding. They have many people to support.

The way of building is based on the owner's idea and also the hand-ink master in the area—whatever his skills and designs are. There can be all kinds of houses. I think that houses in this area are the best cases for architectural design, even if you compare them to those in the city. Every type of house can be found here. Some of them are restored. Some of them are newly built.

When I was studying in the city, I saw the towers and villas: different ways of living. I had the thought that I wanted to earn money so that I could build such a house. Everyone thinks like this when they return from the city. And so, when they get back, they start to build different kinds of houses.

People here are farmers. They can do all kinds of work, including building. In a way, they don't need to spend money to hire designers. They make the designs themselves. Farmers in the city are working in buildings designed by designers. Every step they walk is along a line in the drawing of a designer. When they get back, they make their houses according to what they learned.

The Terrace Farmer, Maogong county, Guizhou province, November 2017.

I farm with my husband. We plant rice, raise pigs, chickens, and ducks. Before, we had more than a hundred ducks. I have been living in the house for 25 years—since I got married. I was 21. I was born here in the village. My husband is from another clan.

Before, my husband's parents had an old house here. But it was taken apart long ago. They had four sons—my husband's parents. They built this house for the eldest son and youngest son, my husband. They built another house for the middle sons. But before the second house, there was a time when all four brothers lived in this house. Two upstairs, two downstairs. It was crowded. But then, the second house was finished, and the middle brothers moved away. The oldest bought their rooms. Later, the oldest also moved out and we bought his rooms. It was then that my husband and I owned the whole house. In the end it was good, because we had three children. We needed all the space.

Before, we were working in Shantou. I was working in a clothing factory and my husband in a bag factory. My husband's parents looked after our three boys. But then my husband returned here to the village when his father, my father-in-law, was sick and could no longer work the fields. Three years ago, the old man died. I stayed in Shantou working in the factory for two more years while my husband farmed my father-in-law's field. We needed the money to pay for the helpers to build a concrete granary. So, I stayed in Shantou.

The house has changed quite a bit. We made it bigger. We added the three-bay space at the back, the basement, and also, as I said, the granary. The kitchen, we built ten years ago. Before, when we shared the house, there were two kitchens. Our kitchen was at the side and my husband's brother's was at the back of the house. But anyway, both kitchens were attached to the house and we closed them with metal sheets. Then, as I said, my husband's brother built a new house and moved. It was then that we took apart the old, attached kitchens. This made it possible to extend the house for a new kitchen and storage.

We built the shower room six or seven years ago. But still there is no water heater. Before, we were washing in that dug-out space in the summer and then, in the winter, in the small yard. The toilet is outside of the house, on the hillside near the road. Before we moved to Shantou, we did not have a gate. I was worried about safety when my husband left the village to work there. I thought it would be safer with a gate.

We made the basement three years ago. It took us a whole year. It was laborious. We excavated the earth with hoes and moved it out on our shoulders and then piled it here. The ground in front of the backdoor was lower before. Now it has been raised. We built the concrete and brick walls too. Before, it was enclosed with iron sheets. But it was not safe and needed to be changed annually. There was a fireplace in the ground, but we replaced it with the stove. It was a fireplace of yellow mud enclosed with iron sheets—like the old kitchens.

Now my oldest son and my second son work as house decorators in Guangzhou. The eldest sometimes sends money back. He will send one or two thousand yuan during the busy times: for example, during the rice harvest. The second one also sends about the same amount. But he is also busy learning. He is learning computer science. But the fee of the program is 5,000 yuan. Since we don't have money to send him, he attends the program with his savings. My third son is working in an electronics factory in Shenzen. But he has only been away several months. He is still asking me for money to pay the train tickets. Sometimes we call on the telephone.

We don't have money to renovate the house anymore. We don't have money to build a new house in the fields near the main road either. I don't think we are capable of it now anyway. Others have built new homes in the fields near the road. They have moved down from the hillside. There are new houses everywhere now. It has grown. Some others bought new houses in the town. But I like living on the hillside. It is close to our fields, making farming and planting vegetables much easier. I cook breakfast after getting up in the morning, and then cook food for the pigs and then feed them. After that I cook lunch. After a break, I go to our fields on the hill to farm. At around 5 or 6 pm I go back home and cook dinner. I watch television in the evening and go to bed after nine.

III. THE COLLECTIVE HOUSE

Multi-story, earthen wall *tulou* have been a part of the southwestern districts of Fujian province for hundreds of years. The continuous construction of these collective dwellings suggests the capacity of the typology to respond to changes in ways of living. The Hakka migrants who originated the *tulou* settled remote areas of Fujian expecting that this isolation would keep them at a welcome distance from populated Han districts. This isolation also instigated the defensive and collective nature of the typology, which secured families from bandits and wild animals. The earliest *tulou* comprised thick stacked stone walls, attesting to this defensive origin. Later, a method of earthen construction that could be completed collectively with little skill predominated.

Since the most recent period of *tulou* construction in the 1970s, Fujian has undergone radical transformations. Many *tulou* are now enveloped by urban sprawl. New infrastructural networks link more remote villages to urban areas and economic opportunity. The 2008 UNESCO World Heritage designation of 46 *tulou* clusters catalyzed preservation discourses and a growing tourist economy around these sites. In other villages, many *tulou* are emptied of residents. Nevertheless, the continued appeal of the *tulou's* collective way of living has led to cases of remarkable adaptation. These innovations hybridize the *tulou's* organizational logic with new spatial ideas. The results reveal the flexibility of the diagram at the *tulou's* core while asserting its capacity to sustain contemporary modes of collective living.

A *tulou* comprises an exterior wall several stories high and one to two meters thick. This wall was typically made of a mixture of earth, glutinous rice, egg whites, and sugar, reinforced with bamboo or fir branches. In the oldest structures, the perimeter was round or oval, but square and rectangular *tulou* are also prevalent, each form determined in relation to the landscape. Wood from the surrounding forests was used for the remaining structure, with large beams supporting floors, partitions, interior walkways, and staircases. Families lived vertically, in stacked rooms looking out onto a central courtyard. A single entrance secured by thick wooden doors reinforced with an iron plate connected the courtyard to the exterior. Winds circulate through the entrance door into the courtyard and the walls absorb heat in the summer. Small windows looking out through the perimeter were reserved for the upper floors.

The collective building of *tulou* was a slow process, with each layer of earth needing time to dry before another could be added. One story could take up to a year. Upon completion, families were allotted one of the identical units through lottery, their ownership comprising shares in a cooperative. These families often carried the same last name—and could only pass on their shares to other family members. As fortunes changed over time, one single *tulou* could house people from multiple economic positions. Another governing rule prevented owners from demolishing their section so that the structural integrity of the whole could be ensured. Stairs and interior passageways were maintained in common. While most courtyards were used for cooking and collective activities, some were filled with single-story structures that housed specific programs: schools, ancestor halls, or stages for festivals and performances. In more recent years, the courtyard in some *tulou* has been divided in radial sections corresponding with each family's living unit and used to build toilets or kitchens.

The *tulou's* spatial diagram is scalable, with the smallest housing ten families and the largest comprising up to several hundred people. This communal mode of living allowed the *tulou* to endure the tumultuous political events of early 20th-century China, when Fujian served as an important terrain for both the Chinese Civil War and the Cultural Revolution. The mixing of class and status within each *tulou* meant there was a solidarity between families; as every family was allotted an identical portion, outsiders had difficulty distinguishing rich land-owners from those families with more meager fortunes. The *tulou*'s dense spatial organization also reserved land for agricultural production in a region where the hilly landscape made cultivable terrain rare.

More recent transformations to economies of labor and material have made the *tulou* less resilient to radical changes to livelihood, family structure, and ways of living. Today, the construction of a traditional *tulou* would cost nearly five times as much as a concrete frame building that housed an equivalent number of people. The wooden beams that connect interior earthen walls need to be sourced and shipped from elsewhere rather than culled in a nearby forest. And the cost of labor, once carried out by residents themselves, quickly makes such a project unviable. Where before family members might be related to everyone within their *tulou*, these consanguineal bonds have been frayed by economic migration and the loosening of rules governing the buying and selling of shares. As families may not reside in their homes for more than a few weeks a year—the only permanent residents being older couples and the very young children left under their guard—collective living is constituted in different ways. Individual counters for electricity and water reveal new comforts and a transformed relationship between the collective and the maintenance of everyday life.

The elements of the *tulou's* diagram—the defensive perimeter, the common courtyard, the hierarchy between earthen-walls and wooden elements—are today reinterpreted to reflect new priorities. Whole sections of *tulou* are remade or completely dismantled, new construction methods making it possible to reinforce the structural integrity of the *tulou's* once inviolate earthen wall. Inhabitants expand their houses outwards, breaking through the perimeter and offering direct access to their units from the street. This allows some families to offer services that respond to the enlarged sphere of economic activity that comprises village life. Other times, construction pushes inward, reinscribing the courtyard with a new character. When space allows, some families choose to build outside the *tulou* itself, with bridges or rooms linking back into the original structure.

These choices are determined collectively, with each *tulou* functioning with its own set of decision-making rules. Some are governed by a rotating leader, while in others, residents make decisions by consensus. Small day-to-day issues are discussed on messaging applications. Important choices are made at meetings organized during festivals when family members return to the village. These decisions—whether to build inwards, outwards, breach the perimeter wall, etc.—contribute to the typology's continued capacity to adapt and reflect a desire to maintain the *tulou* as part of a transformed way of life.

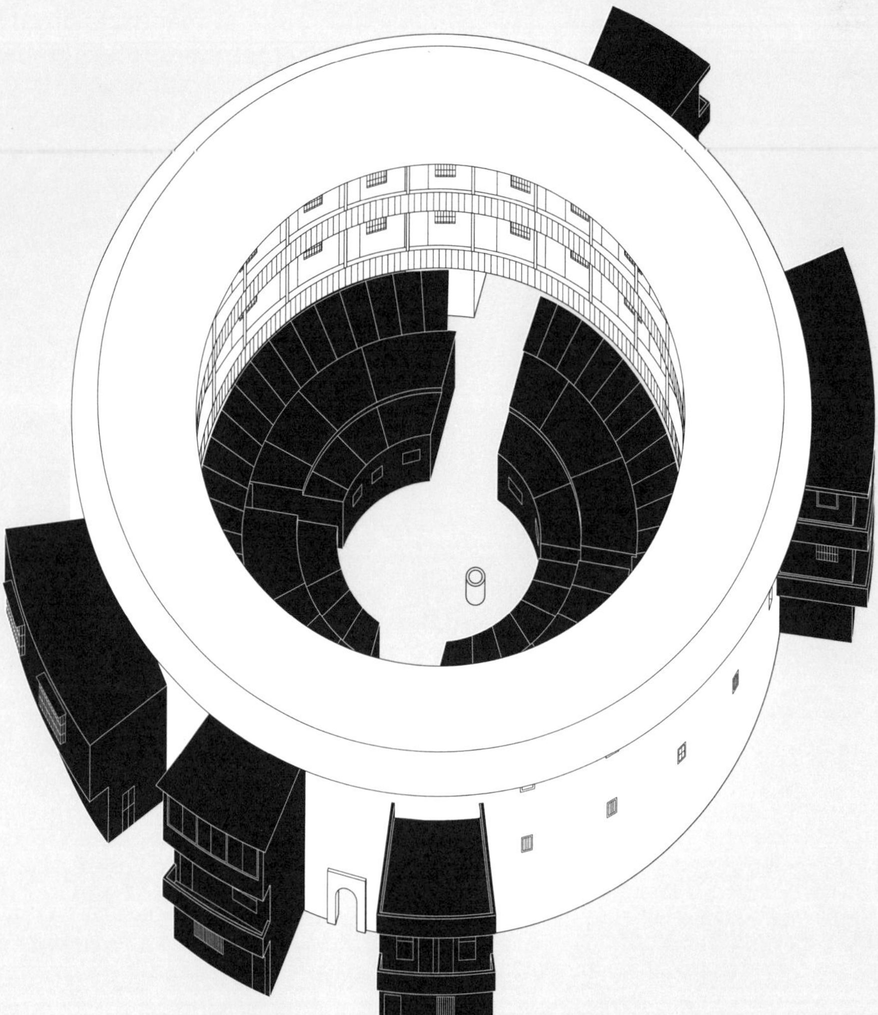

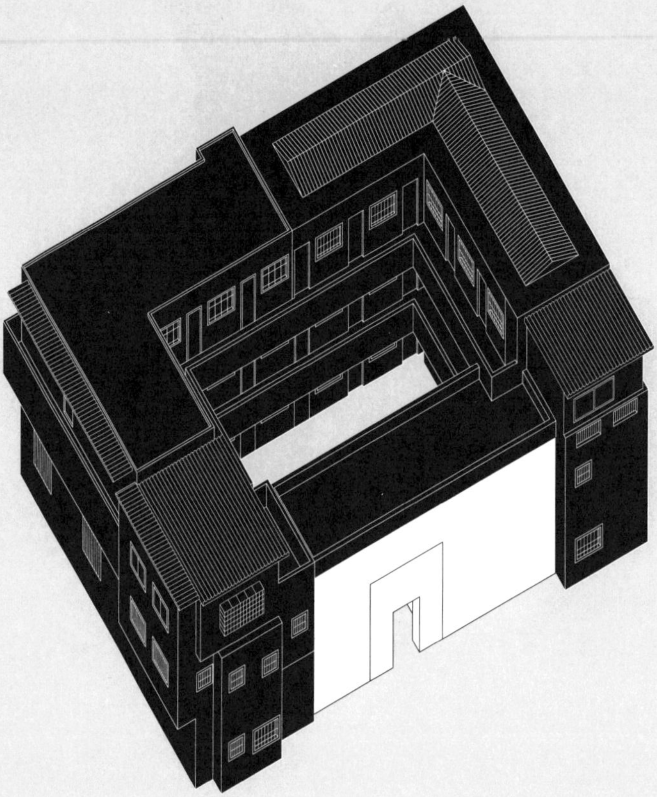

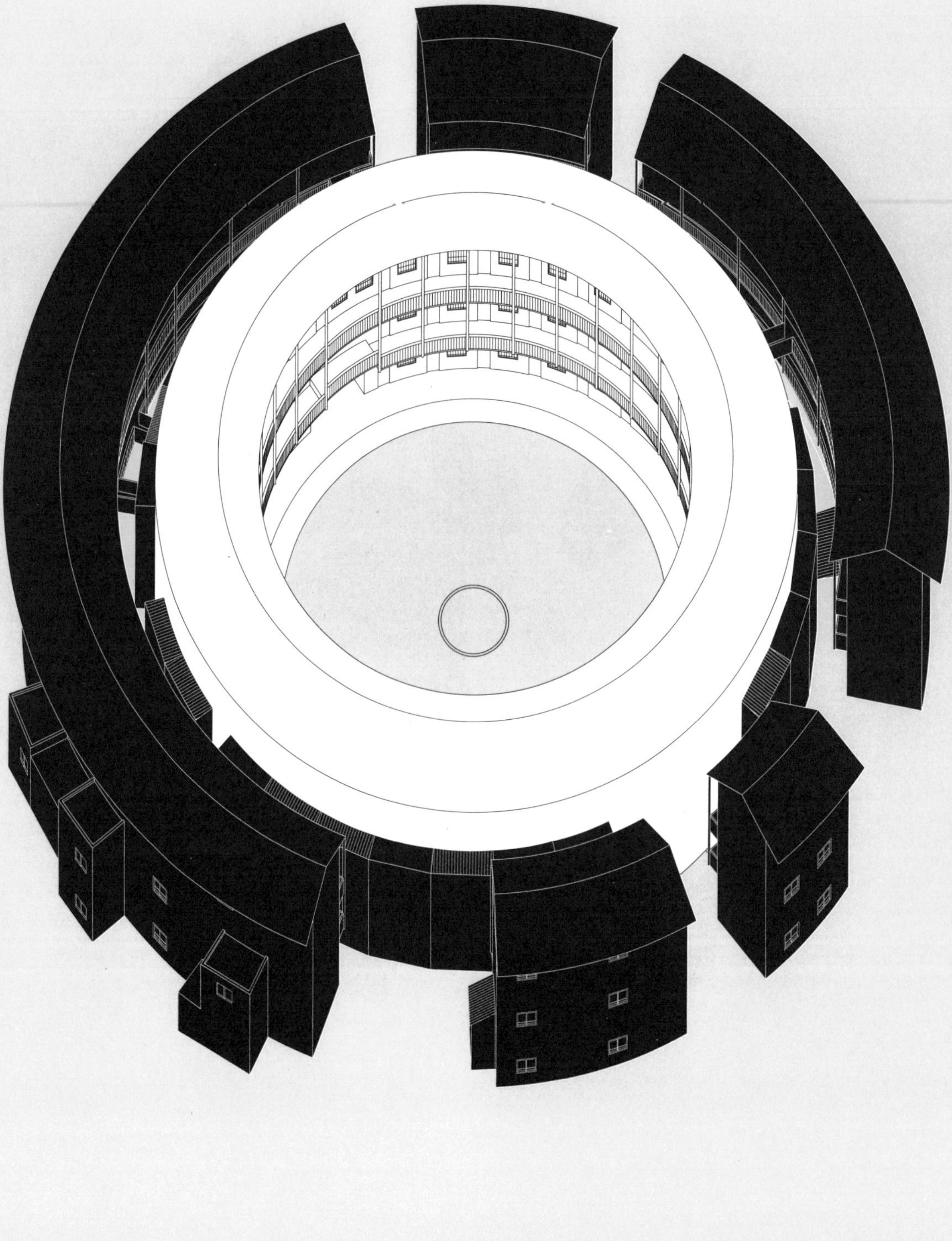

普及防骗知识铭记

蓝田村溢庆楼裔孙第四届盛会合影留念
裕慶樓
二零一五年正月初三日

兰田村溢庆楼裔孙第三届盛会合影留念
2012年正月初三日
兰田村溢庆楼裔孙第二届盛会留念
2011年正月初三日
第五届

PLUG-IN HOUSE

Over the course of several years, this old *tulou* was redefined by additions both inside and outside its wall. The families here wanted to remain part of the traditional collective living structure, but also to have bigger, updated houses. Volumes plugged in to the *tulou* from the exterior, orient their once inward-looking units outward. New openings in the earthen wall link the old spaces to those of the plug-in extensions. The residents can either access their houses through the collective courtyard or from individual street-facing entrances. The plug-in volumes do not have interior stairs. When residents want to travel to an upper room, they must pass through the *tulou's* earthen wall and take a communal staircase, before passing back through the wall to the space above. Each family was also attributed an equal, radially delimited slice within the courtyard in front of their unit. They developed these spaces into individual additions housing bathrooms and kitchens. Some residents covered the gap between the entrance to their house and the new courtyard additions with a polycarbonate awning supported on a steel frame. This translucid covering allows them to use the collective space in front of their ground floor rooms all year. Outdoor stoves, baskets, basins, and benches are neatly organized in this space. Despite the courtyard additions, there is still sufficient space for all 30 families to gather there for festival celebrations.

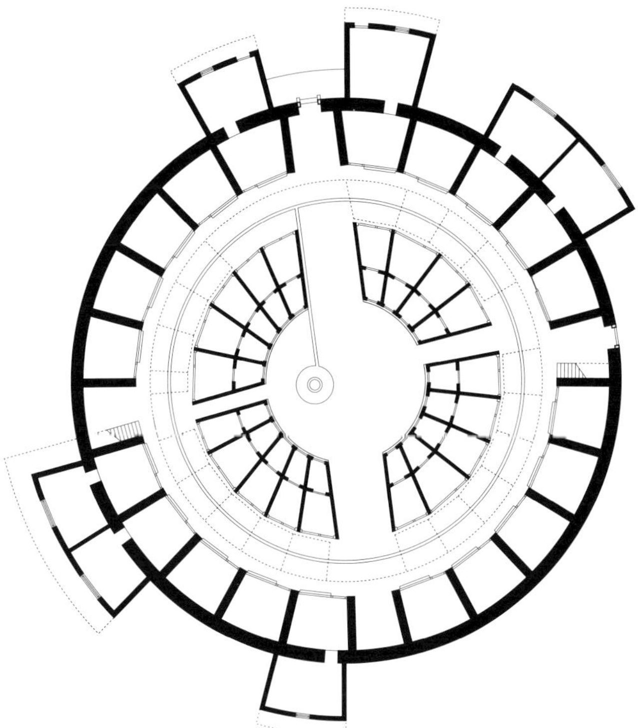

0 2m

家接富貴好運來
福

一帆風順
全家和順泰百福
內外平安好運
吉星永照富貴門

OUTSIDE IN HOUSE

A small village of new constructions was hidden behind the thick earthen walls of this *tulou*. Three families each built individual houses to replace their original *tulou* sections. These three- to five-story concrete frame buildings replaced walls, walkways, floors, and stairs all made from wood. The additions project into the courtyard up to an agreed-upon limit that marks the division between family ownership and the shared communal space. Despite the changes inside, the exterior wall has been almost unaltered. The residents decided collectively to maintain the *tulou's* traditional external appearance. The more radical changes within have encouraged families to return to the *tulou* more often, during auspicious festivals, for example. Some older residents chose to live in the new additions, while others preferred to stay in their traditional units. Before the transformation, balconies lined the *tulou's* inner perimeter, forming a continuous walkway overlooking the regular square courtyard. Residents in any corner could quickly survey nearly every dwelling. With the new, projecting concrete additions, intimate spaces, and hidden corners allow for different types of informal encounters and activities.

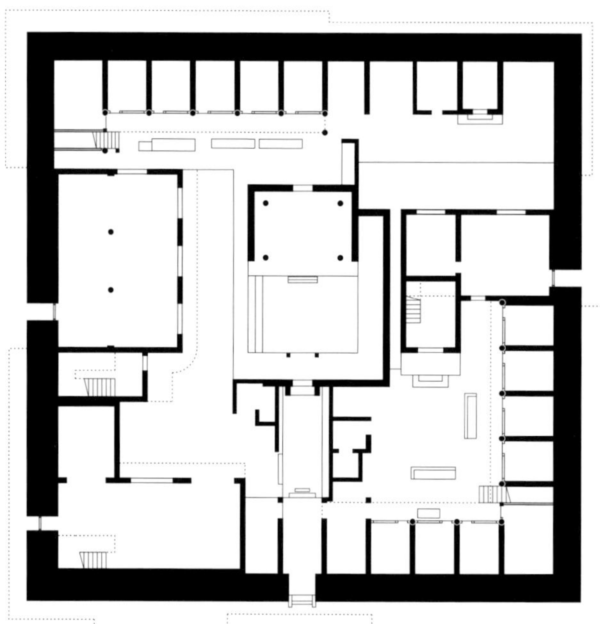

0 2m

福到财来千秋盛

REMAKE HOUSE

Eight brothers remade their inherited sections one after the other, recreating a collective inhabitation. The *tulou* is relatively small, with a narrow rectangular courtyard. The brothers replaced each of their portions of the original *tulou* with a two-story construction, finished in its own cladding or color. Nevertheless, the remade sections respected the *tulou's* original circulation and footprint. From the outside, the building is barely recognizable as a *tulou*. Only the mud entrance wall from the original structure has been maintained. The rooms of this original earthen fragment have been left unenclosed and are used for storage. When the brothers needed more space, they decided to add an additional story to their houses. They flattened the roof of the remaining earthen fragment, so that it could be used as a terrace by the newly adjacent rooms. To unify the front facade, a thick orange band runs continuously along the edge of the slab. The courtyard's proportions are compressed by the additional story. Each corner of the building has its own character, expressed through a particular choice of tiles, decorative features, or paint. The family's different choices within this process of renewal have rendered the *tulou's* system of vertical ownership legible. Although the building is almost entirely rebuilt, it still carries this central idea.

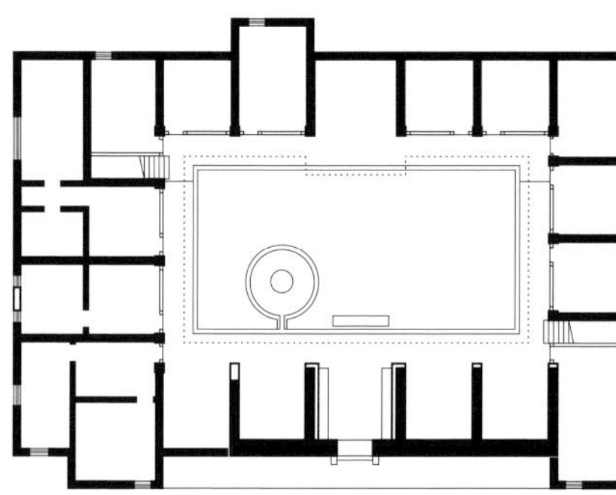

0 2m

SLICE HOUSE

More than half of the original *tulou* was demolished. In the space of the razed structure, families have built free-standing towers whose footprints are defined by the limits of their original allotted slice. The heights of these new constructions vary; some families added extra floors so that their new homes look down onto the roof of the remaining original *tulou* fragments. Other residents abandoned their units and allowed relatives to tear down unused sections to use the land for gardening. Like the new constructions, the gardens also abide by the footprint of the original owner's share of the *tulou*. These garden plots merge with the patchwork of surrounding fields. While the structural integrity of *tulou* once depended on the continuity of the perimeter wall, new ways of building make it possible for sections to exist on their own. One of the remaining *tulou* sections has new brick columns that extend its entire height. Framed views of the surroundings are visible through the new constructions, with the introverted world of the courtyard now open and revealed to the village around it. While retaining the vertical and radial allocation of ownership, this process of patchwork demolition and renewal demonstrates new possibilities for *tulou* development.

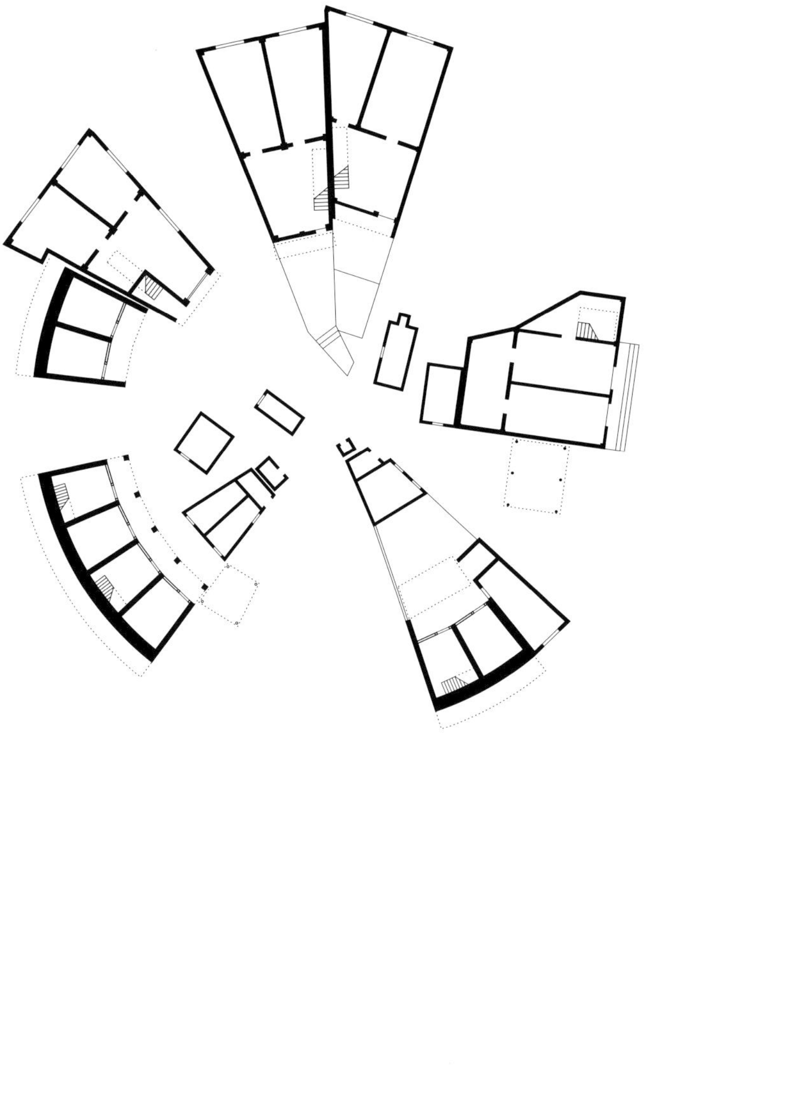
0 2m

DOUBLE HOUSE

The households of this *tulou* received compensation from the regional government when a portion of their farmland was cut away by the construction of a highway. With this compensation, they decided to expand their living spaces. Not wanting to build inwards or teardown the perimeter wall, a second ring of rooms was added around the original *tulou*, extending each family unit outwards. As with the original *tulou*, the new ring is made of rammed earth and wood—a nearly perfect twin of the old structure it circumscribes. In the space between the old and new *tulou* is an alley crisscrossed by bridges that connect upper floor units from the inner and outer buildings. Each family's main living space is generally on the ground floor of the old building; a door leading into the alley and through another entrance sometimes connects to a storage area in the new ring where families keep farming equipment or a space for parking. The upper floors of the *tulou* are typically bedrooms, and the top-most story is used for harvested potatoes, grains, and roots. Kitchens and bathrooms have been added directly to the outer wall of the inner ring and are accessible from outside. These additions, projecting into the alley, ensure that this in-between space is always active. While the central courtyard provides a place to work or gather, the alley allows for more informal encounters. The double house is a collectively conceived, large-scale strategy for expansion.

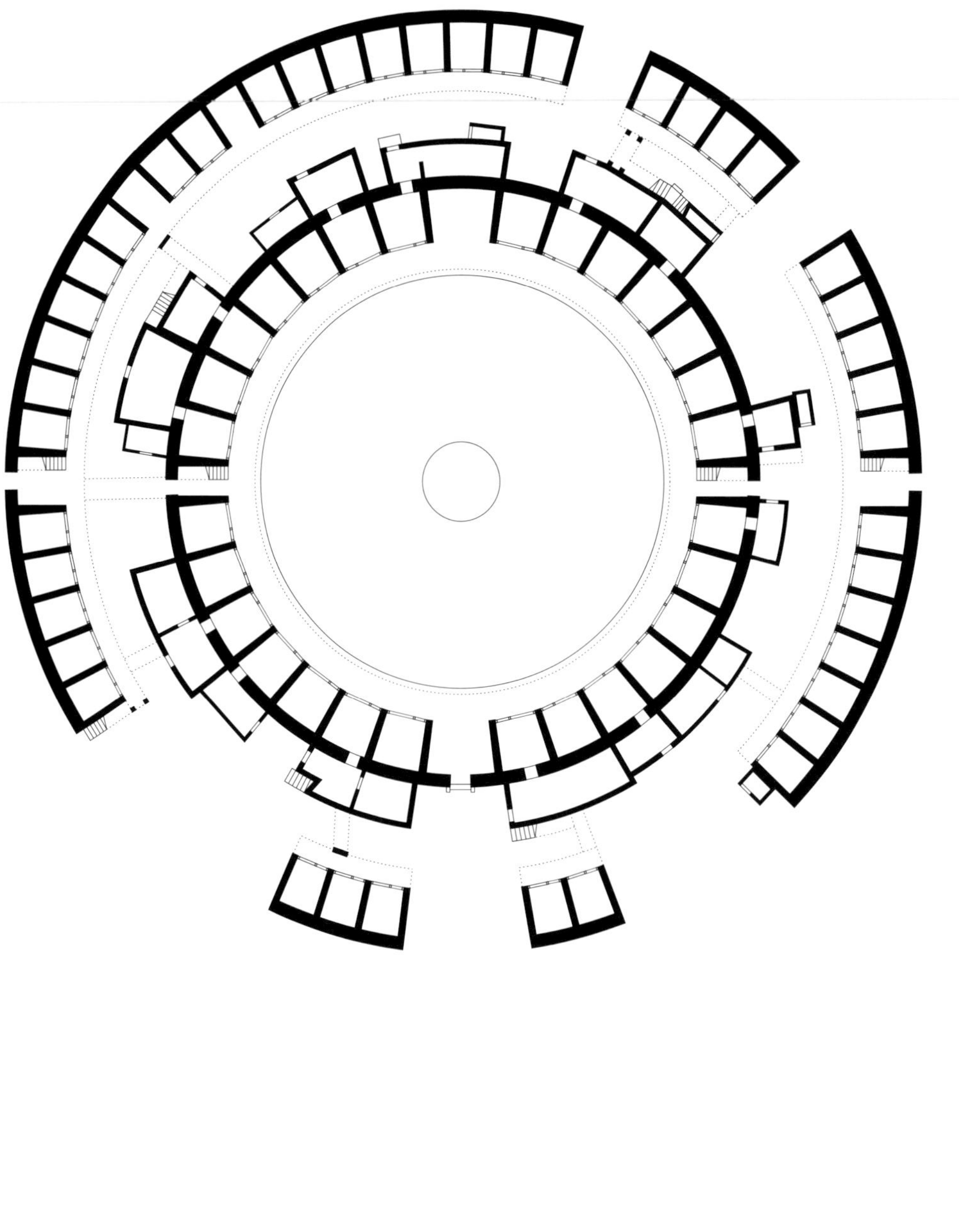
0 2m

一帶春風一路歌
萬事如意
福

The Medicine Giver, outside of Xiamen, in Fujian province, June 2018.

Most of the people here have the surname Jiang. I grew up in Fuzhou and my husband grew up here. His parents moved here when he was young and bought this land. A lot of people used to buy land then. My husband grew up in this *tulou*. Then I moved in.

There was a *tulou* in ruins on this land, which had burned before the Cultural Revolution. Forty years ago, we were able to buy and renovate a small part that was not destroyed in the fire. After we got married and after the birth of my first son, we rebuilt the *tulou*. Before that, we lived in a place assigned to us during the land reformation, but that place collapsed long ago. My sons and grandchildren all grew up here. They are teenagers now, my grandchildren. Their parents had to work, so they were unable to take care of them. They stayed here with us so they could go to the elementary and high schools nearby. But in the end, they had rather poor grades. Now, they go to school in the city. Schools are better in the city. The oldest is 19, the younger one is 12, and the youngest is seven. But they do not need me to look after them. They can look after themselves. My granddaughter is in the fifth grade, studying in Xiamen. She called me to tell me that she got a score of 100 for math and a score of 93 for Chinese.

I have one daughter and two sons. One son is in Xiamen and another son is in Guangzhou. My daughter is in Shenzhen. I do not know what jobs they do. Even if they told me what they do, I wouldn't understand. I haven't visited them because I prefer not to do long journeys. They rarely come home. Only for Chinese New Year—around four or five days a year.

I like living here. The air quality is great. There are now three families in the *tulou*. The other families began their renovations a few years after us. We were a few years early. We had to build the roof at the same time as the other parts, or else the structure would have collapsed. It had to be attached together. Each family took on the design and construction of their own parts, but we had to discuss the connection of the roof together. I built first, and their parts were supported by my part of the roof. The *tulou* has three stories. Each family has its own staircase. Three in total. We do not share the staircases like in the old *tulou*.

All the rooms are very messy. I put everything in the rooms, including logs and whatnot. It is not as neat and empty as rooms in the city. When we first moved here, there was only electricity on the outside of the *tulou*; now it's inside. The kitchen is now inside too. There are two rooms for the kitchen; it wraps around the staircase at the corner. We added a glass door that was not there before, because of the smell of the waste water from the septic tank and petrol from cars. Today there are only a few residents: mostly old women, me, and my husband. My husband and I are both retired. I am 67 years old and my husband is 70-something. During the day I cook. Sometimes I farm vegetables on our land and do house chores. We get a pension for our retirement. It is not that much: about 4,000 yuan per person. My husband is a doctor and still sees patients. Before he retired, he worked at the county hospital. That was more than ten years ago when he was 62. Now he sees patients here at home. Sometimes, when my husband treats patients I give them medicine.

But I was a farmer. I have always been doing farm work. Today, we do not have much land for farming. This is a very mountainous region, so already there was very little land. The good land we did have was developed for roads. The government paid us, but very little: around 800 yuan. One square meter of land was only two or three yuan back then. We had no say over the development. The government wanted to build highways and a secondary school. They renovate the roads all the time. But the school is not in use today. No one goes to school here anymore. There used to be over 2,000 students, but now there are only around 200. The other children have all been sent to the city.

These days we get very few visitors. There were more last year. I earned thousands of yuan last year, but none this year. I would sell cigarettes, tea leaves, *longan*, things like that. I bought them and then resold them; we cannot plant those things here. The tourists come in groups. Sometimes there are up to 20,000 visitors a year. This year—I am not sure why—there aren't any visitors. Maybe they've come and seen it all already. There is nothing much to see here. Nothing special. There are a lot of mosquitoes, flies, and insects, but our place is very clean.

I have two chickens. When my granddaughter comes back, we plan to kill them. My chickens know that I am their owner and they stay in my area. I also have a small vegetable garden. And then by the bridge, there is a small store. It is not quite new, but it sells cigarettes and alcohol, and groceries like salt, sugar, and soy sauce. I can get what I need there. It is near the new village which was built on farmland seven to ten years ago. This area used to be filled with *tulou*, but no one lives in them anymore. It is a pity how they are all vacant now.

In the afternoon, I just lie here. I go to bed at around 10 pm. In the morning, I have to wake up early: around 5 am. If I cannot fall asleep, I get up.

Madame Li, outside of Xiamen, in Fujian province, June 2018.

When *tulou* were declared World Heritage sites, an officer from UNESCO came to visit. He told us: "*Tulou* are 'full stops' that, unearthed, lead to countless 'question-marks' and 'exclamation marks.'" He also said that *tulou* are like an encyclopedia that can never be fully comprehended. They embody vast knowledge ranging from *Feng Shui*, architecture, aesthetics, environmental science, anthropology, topology, and landscape. According to the masters, the *tulou* must echo the *Feng Shui* of its surrounding area. It is not up to us to decide, as the traditional study of *Feng Shui* is rather profound and cannot be easily understood. There are rectangular *tulou* and circular ones. The square or rectangular *tulou* represents flat "land," while a circular one represents "sky." It takes a long time to build a *tulou*. One with four floors can take 16 years from planning to the completion of building.

In the past, many landlords were extremely wealthy. Some were even governors. They often had officers or visitors of higher social standing come to visit them at the *tulou*. In the courtyard, there might be an independent building that served as a hostel, for example, with a performance stage and dining area on the ground floor and guest rooms on the second floor.

Some of the most impressive *tulou* are divided into eight equal parts. This is based on the Eight Trigrams—also from *Feng Shui*. The very famous Prince of Tulou in Hongkeng village was built this way. Now it is quite popular with tourists. The nation's president also requested to visit in person! It has eight staircases with eight units, each separated with a door. If you want to divide or connect between the units you need only to close the door. Every unit also has brick partitions from the first to the fourth floor that serve as firewalls. As *tulou* are mainly built with mud and wood, these can be quite important. You see, the construction of *tulou* is scientific. In the *tulou* itself, the first floor served as kitchen space, and the second to the fourth floor consisted of bedrooms. The layout is truly impressive.

The *tulou* around here are 70 to 80 years old. The oldest one—a rectangular one—is more than 100 years old. No one lives there anymore: only ducks and chickens, fleas, and spider webs. It is very dirty. I do not dare go inside. The owners abandoned it. The longer these buildings are vacant, the higher the risk of them collapsing. If people lived in the *tulou*, they would be repaired regularly. Otherwise, they wear out easily in a few years when problems like a leaking ceiling occur. Villages are like this. We have too much land, but no one wants it. Maybe it is worth a lot of money too, since the government refuses to approve land for building houses now.

My eldest daughter studies IT: information technology. When she was deciding her field of study, I told her that this is a profession for guys. "Why do you want to do this?" She took six mathematics and science classes in high school. And I asked her what specialty she was interested in and she told me that she could not make the decision until year two in college. Everything I say, she tells me: "Mom, you do not understand." I really don't! I can only provide them with the financial support they need. I just tell her that she must study hard. My son studies the same field in Xiamen. My daughter's registered residence is with my husband's family, whereas my son is registered here. But it does not worry me. Once my daughter meets someone in college and gets married, her registered residence will change anyway.

We are all descendants of the same family. Everyone who lives in this *tulou* shares the surname Li. Before, everyone in the village had the same surname. That is how it used to be; today, that is no longer the case. There are too many surnames to keep track of now. Houses are too commercialized, often sold and bought. That is why the residents vary so much, similar to Hong Kong. In some of the new buildings, residents have all types of surnames.

Before, all the rooms of the *tulou* were crowded, filled with families. Now, all together, there are three families here. Everyone else has moved out even though the houses still belong to them. Most have moved to newer houses. Some bought houses in the city, the others moved to other buildings around this area. The ones who went to the city leave the older ones and the children behind. The younger ones need to go to school, while the older ones take care of them. Then finally, it is only the older ones who are left. This is what happens in the villages.

IV.

THE SEASONAL HOUSE

Tibetan families have lived in northwestern Yunnan province for generations, farming lands that are 3,000 meters above sea level. Around the city of Xianggelila, also known as Shangri-La, many of these farmers have moved into developing peri-urban districts to be closer to the city. The farmers build houses that replicate traditional rural architecture and adapt them for modern life. These adaptations have been singularly influenced by the adoption of glass and steel construction, transforming outdoor courtyards into year-round spaces warmed by the sun. The proliferation of glass and steel has, in turn, transformed the way local builders conceive of the farmhouse itself.

Traditional farmhouses use rammed earth and timber construction in a spatial configuration that unifies the exterior space of an enclosed courtyard with the house. Each farmstead comprises an outer perimeter wall that, on one end of the compound, becomes the outer wall of the house itself. A recessed porch acts as a transition between the ground floor of the house and the courtyard; animals ranged freely between these spaces to keep warm in the harsh winters. The family lived upstairs on the first floor, where the interior spaces are defined by a grid of large timber columns raised on stone bases. Windowless interior rooms are enclosed by finely carved wooden partitions. To keep warm during the long winters, families would gather in these introverted spaces around cooking ovens. Paneling on the earthen walls further insulates the space. The top-most floor of the farmhouse, used to store the harvest, was covered by a shallow pitched roof supported on wooden trusses. The trusses rested on the massive earthen wall, so that the roof itself seems to be floating.

As families moved closer to the edge of the city and the government provided incentives for raising new types of crops, the subsistence farming that defined their livelihoods became less appealing. Farmers began growing expensive varieties of mushrooms or other seasonal cash crops that would quickly go to market. New rules that required animals to be kept in separate structures outside of the main house accelerated the abandonment of animal husbandry that had been an integral part of the rural homestead. With these changes to livelihood, residents began to adapt the spatial organization of their houses.

New, reliable road connections to Chengdu to the northeast and Kunming to the south gave the region access to contractors, laborers, and industrial materials, and with them, methods that were cheaper and quicker than traditional ways of building. The most influential of these ideas was the use of glass and steel to address climatic conditions. Extreme temperatures in summer and winter are characterized by clear skies and abundant sun; due to the region's high altitude, sunrays are intense and heat dissipates more quickly from the earth.

Early building experiments addressed these issues by using cheap glass and steel construction to enclose the recessed ground-floor porch. With the addition of a glass screen to act as a thermal buffer, the winter sun heats the enclosed space. This trapped heat then radiates to other rooms within the house. In the winter months, as temperatures fall below freezing, the new room is warmed by the sun. In the summer, adjustable panes and blinds are used to regulate temperatures. These first experiments with glass and steel led to increasingly ambitious constructions. Families enclosed more of the courtyard space until soon it was entirely covered with a glass and steel shed, creating a tempered environment that provided new possibilities for use. In space that was previously reserved for animals and the storage of farm equipment, families install elaborate gardens made up of fountains, plants, and shaded sitting areas; chandeliers are often found hanging from the trusses that hold up the glass roof. Other families use the tempered space for storing firewood, hanging laundry, keeping plants, or simply extending their living space into the new year-round environment.

Material for these constructions can easily be ordered from the nearby cities, with contractors in Xianggelila quickly developing a building competence of their own. Soon, the idea spread from household to household, with minor alterations depending on needs, costs, and personal preference. Families replaced the glass with synthetic panels that were easier to seal, more structurally efficient, and could be integrated with films to screen UV rays or sunlight. Today, the structural frame holding the transparent panes is often made from industrially produced elements sized for efficiency. Some components are assembled at the factory, but installation often requires welding and measurement on-site to account for the anomalies in traditional construction. The popularity of these architectural additions is such that in the city and its outskirts, glass volumes are densely scattered across the hillsides.

Construction of the glass volumes requires less investment than the costs associated with building a traditional house. Today, the earth for walls and the timber for columns can no longer be sourced in the region; families wanting to build traditionally travel to Myanmar or southern Yunnan to find individual timber logs. Because of these difficulties, some families combine generic building materials and methods with the traditional farmhouse typology to create hybrid constructions: concrete frame, brick-infill structures, fronted by courtyards and enclosed by perimeter walls that introduce contemporary ideas of domesticity into the traditional farmhouse. In these new hybrids, the glass enclosure is not an afterthought but is part of the initial house design. This integrated approach means that the interior spaces of the house are also influenced by the glass enclosure. While there may still be traditional rooms lined with dark paneling and oriented toward interior family life, other spaces take advantage of the sunlight and offer views of the landscape.

For Tibetan families, house-building is the primary object of investment. Any new or unexpected income is immediately put back into construction. Sons are expected to leave their parents' home and build a house of their own, even if the new residence is adjacent. Construction can take several years, with each year's net income used to continue building in those months when the weather allows. Yet, even once a house is completed, families invest in improvements, alterations, or new additions. Building an entirely new house with the arrival of money is also not unusual. It is perhaps this specific dynamic that has catalyzed building experiments in the region. The rapid proliferation of glass and steel structures is the most visible example of this dynamic; in their representation of changes to livelihood and domesticity, they have transformed the landscape, affording new ways of living and prototypes that are in dialogue with the still present spatial ways of tradition.

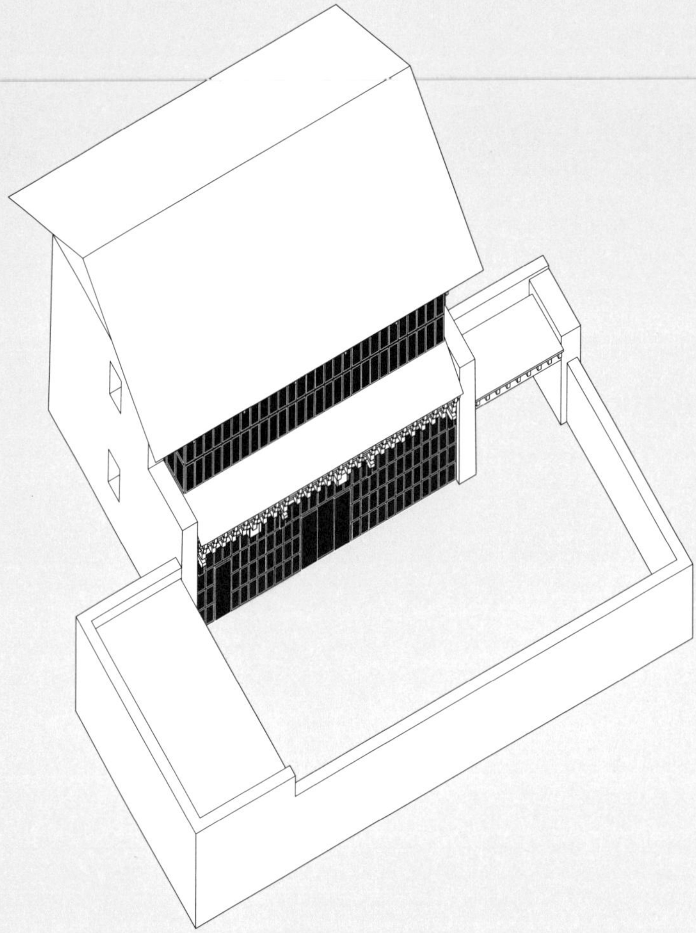

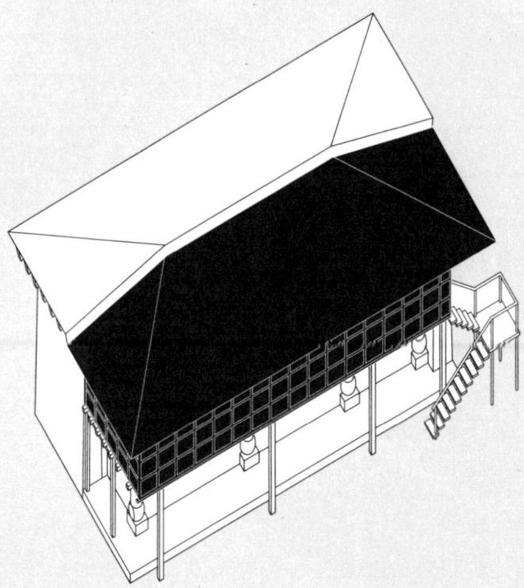

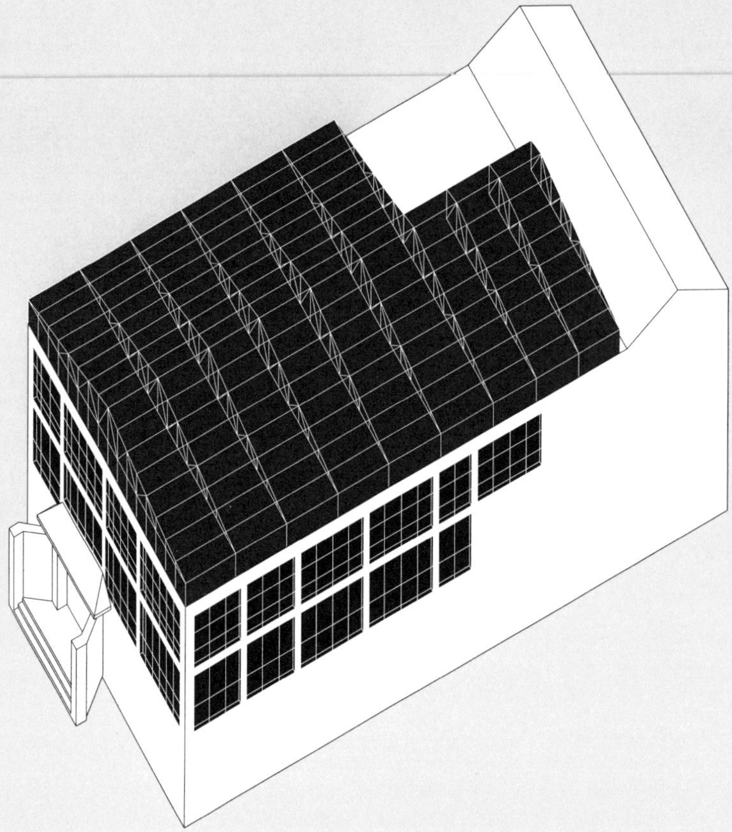

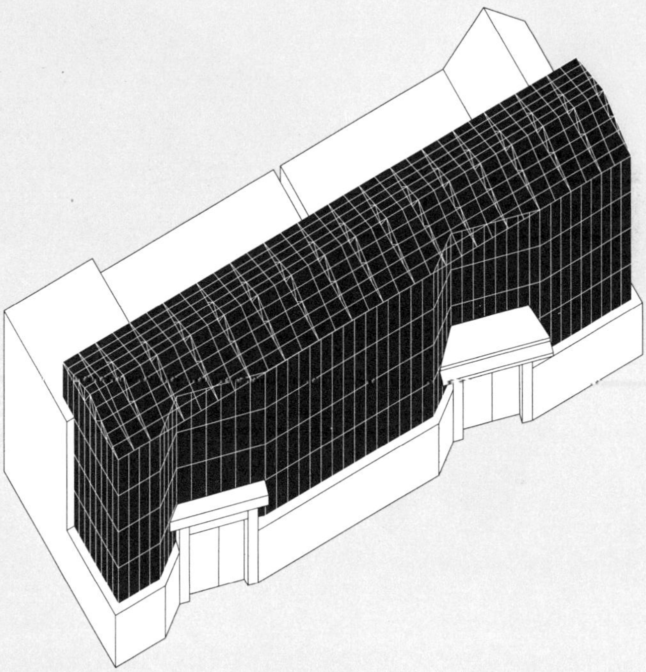

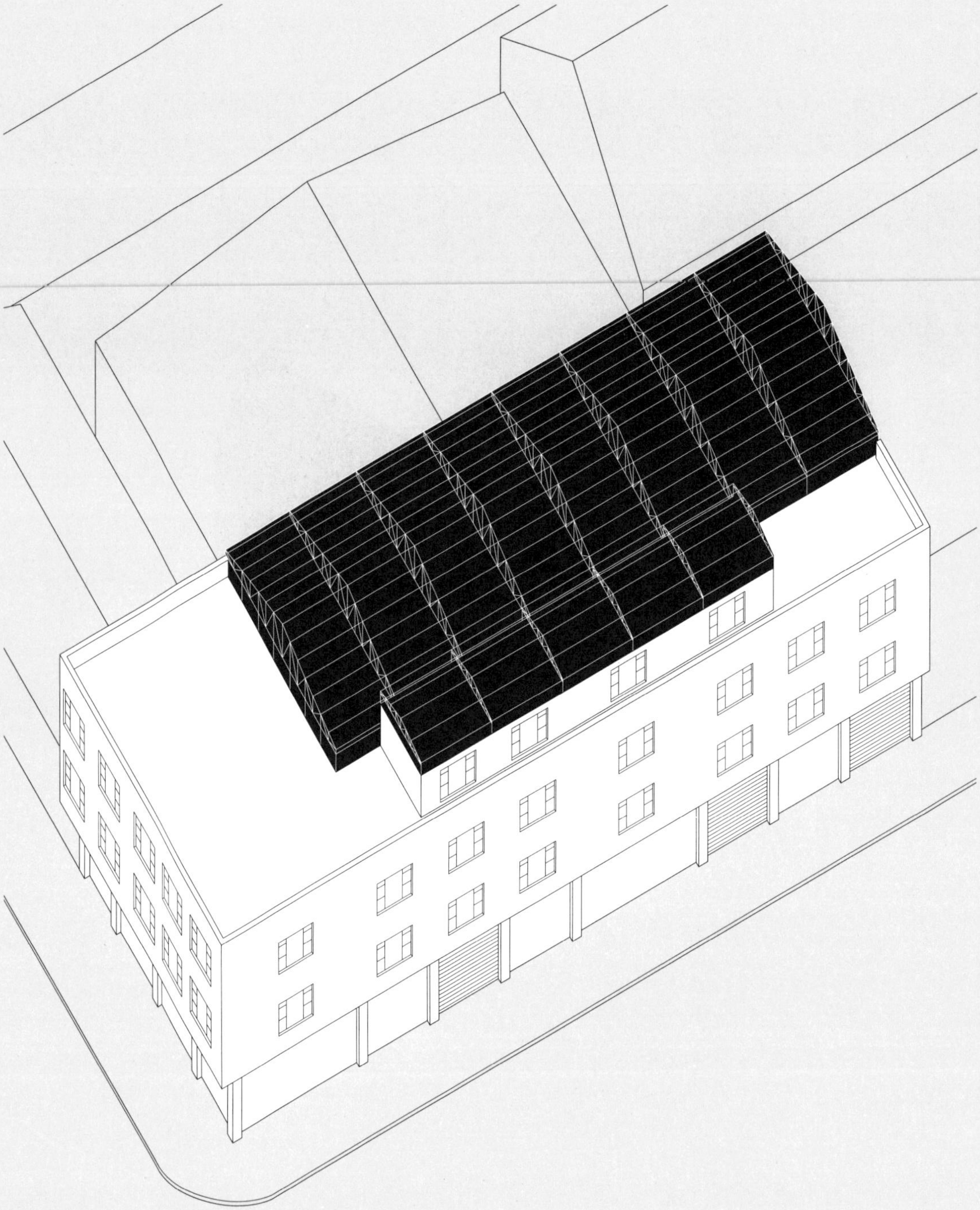

云R·36436

FLAT FACADE HOUSE

Ten years ago, this house was the first in the village to use a glass facade. The thick outer perimeter wall is made from rammed earth. Inside, columns the size of tree-trunks and warm, carved wood cladding create a domestic interior that contrasts with the more barren exterior landscape. The house faces southward; a porch running its length opens into a walled-in yard that is surrounded by fields. The family decided to take advantage of this orientation and the strong sunlight that entered the porch during winter months; they enclosed the porch with a continuous plane of single glazing. The finely crafted, tree-size columns that begin in a row on the porch and continue into the house are now masked by the grid of glass. Later, they enclosed an upper floor balcony in nearly the same way, so that the entire southern facade reflects sunlight throughout the day. The new enclosed spaces store heat that radiates to the rest of the house in the winter. Initially, the ground floor facade only had two openings for doors. To allow for warm air to better circulate in the summer, some fixed glazing was replaced with openable windows. With these minimal additions to the facade of their house, the owners created an environmental prototype.

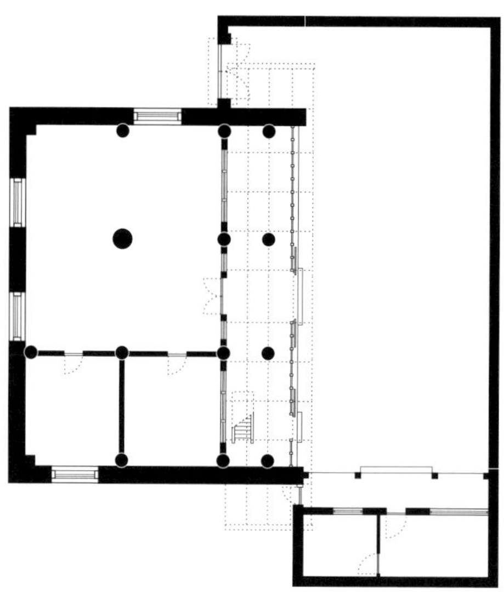

0 2m

HALF AND HALF HOUSE

To be closer to the highway, the family moved their traditional house from a nearby hillside to a new location at the edge of the city. While it was not possible to displace the earthen wall of the old structure, they salvaged four massive columns, as well as carved wooden partitions and interior cladding. On the new, smaller site, the owners built a two-story, C-shaped earthen wall that would be half of the new house. Within the space defined by the wall, they enclosed traditional rooms with wooden partitions. On the upper floor, the perimeter of the three-sided earthen construction is mirrored by a glass and steel volume, supported in the air by four slender *pilotis*. Arriving from the street, the entrance passage is defined on one side by these slim steel supports, and on the other by wooden columns engaged into a carved partition wall. Behind this partition is a low space where the family kept goats before the city banned domestic animal husbandry; now the space is used for cooking. At the end of the passage is a steel scissor stair that leads to the glass and steel addition. Nested within the light-filled volume is a room defined by carved-wood partition walls and the columns moved from the original hillside house. A generous space separates this interior room from the glass facade. Since the rebuilding of this house, the owners have erected another residence in the lot next door. It is larger and more traditional in design. But the family still returns to the older house to cook downstairs and spend time above. The glass-enclosed space is warmer than any of the rooms in their new residence.

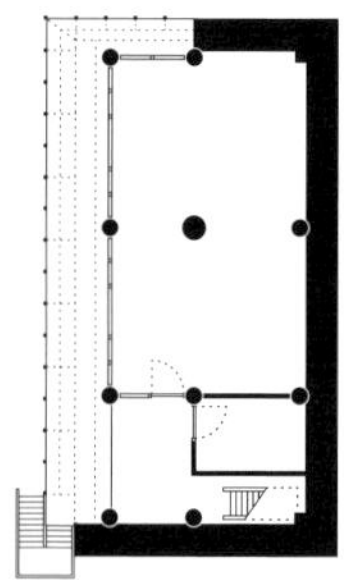
0 2m

HOUSE IN HOUSE

A three-story perimeter wall encloses a landscaped front yard and a newly built house on the outskirts of the city. The high wall is interrupted by a grid of glazed openings that allow views outwards from the yard. Perched on top of the perimeter is a shallow pitched roof comprising a series of steel trusses supporting translucent fiberglass reinforced polyester panels. Affixed to the front of the wall is a carved stone entrance portal crowned with a traditional upturned roof; the lateral arms of the entrance frame stairs and a double door. Inside, the family has decorated the stone-tiled yard with a wooden pergola surrounded by fruit trees; a chandelier hangs from one of the trusses. From this space, another facade appears: a house inside the house. Clad with brick-sized tiles, this second facade recalls suburbs that could be anywhere in the world. The stepped-back volume of the interior house allows for multiple terraces. The largest terrace on the top floor, just below the roof, is furnished with sofas, a canopy swing, a mahjong table, and retractable sunshades. Within the house, the rooms are lined with the dark, carved wood panels that characterize traditional Tibetan domesticity.

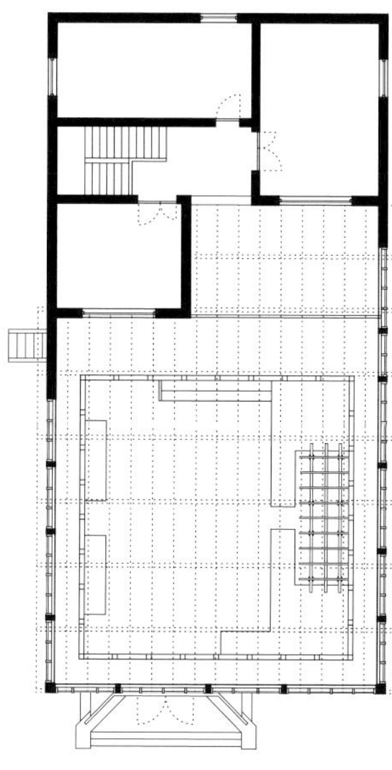

0 2m

ONE ROOF, TWO HOUSES

In a now dense neighborhood on the outskirts of the city, two brothers built individual houses next to one another. Despite being completed at different times, the houses are almost replicas. A shallow courtyard, protected from the narrow street by a boundary wall, runs the length of the two houses and is split into two by a *parti*-wall. Each brother has his own private entrance to his twinned house. With the neighborhood's development, and tall constructions towering over their own, the brothers decided to enclose their courtyards in glass. Instead of building two glass sheds with distinct structural systems, the brothers commissioned the construction of a single roof. On the street side, the shed's steel structure runs along the inner face of the boundary wall and is founded into the ground of a narrow planting area. Where it meets the houses, the shed follows their outline to create an airtight seal. Supporting, horizontal cross-arms anchored to the houses and fixed to the shed structure, protect against strong winter winds. The shared *parti*-wall was rebuilt to incorporate a glass screen between the courtyards. At its height, the screen ends at the lower element of the truss that holds up the pitched roof. The gap formed by the truss allows air to circulate within the shared roof structure. Voices also carry from one courtyard to another. With the addition of the unifying roof, the two small houses claim space for living within the city.

福星高照四季平安全家福

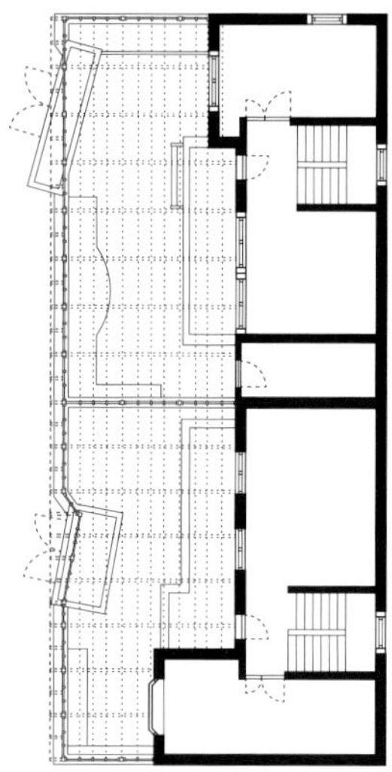

0 2m

HIDDEN HOUSE

When this family relocated to the city, they bought a corner plot in an urban block. The multi-story, L-shaped building they developed on the site defined a rear courtyard space that they covered with a glass and steel structure. Outward-facing units on the ground floor have been leased to shops and offices. Upstairs, small apartments are rented to single workers and also look onto the street. The family home, which looks inward to the courtyard, is accessed through a discreet door from the busy street. Through the door is an unadorned corridor that leads to the light-filled rear yard. Greenery, chandeliers, and an indoor fountain decorate this vast space. Above, white awnings provide shade and privacy to terraced balconies that open from individual bedrooms. On the ground floor, the family sometimes gathers in a room lined with carved wood paneling to watch television or, in the winters, keep warm around a central stove. Two floors above is a sunroom situated between a pitched roof of transparent panels and a tiled floor of structural glass. Clerestory windows in the low-slung, narrow space reveal views of the hills that surround the city. The house exemplifies the ways in which the forces of urbanization are transforming traditional spaces of living. The street-facing commercial activities generate income for the family to live in this new private dreamworld.

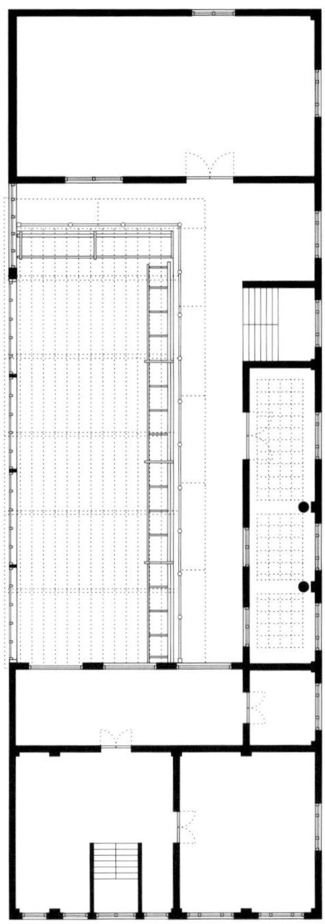

0 2m

The Mushroom Farmer, near Songzanlin monastery, Xianggelila, Yunnan province, January 2018.

We had an open courtyard before, but after the neighbours built their houses, we no longer had direct sunlight. That is why we enclosed the front courtyard. We will renovate the back side after the New Year. It is a bit too cold now and the construction team doesn't work during the winter. I am doing the renovations for my mother. She says in case she passes away, we need a mourning hall. Of course, I don't like hearing her say that. I don't want to follow her suggestion. But anyway I will build a place for that just in case.

Before, if people had more money, they would hold these kind of events outside. For example, they would hold weddings in a restaurant. But now people think the restaurants don't have good food. So we hold these events in the village or in the house. But it takes a lot of energy. We have to help each other with cooking and preparation for three or four days. A lot of effort. We have to help with washing in freezing water.

The house belongs to my second brother. He is the one in charge. He is the vice-director of the hospital. There are four of us living here. I feel a bit embarrassed to end up here. But I didn't want to fall in love with a man. I find men are a bit bossy and they consider themselves always right. Usually if they don't go to school, women here will get married at 17 or 18. Before, there was not so much late marriage. But now we have it: single people who are older. If they focus on their work, they will get married later. I think for traditional Tibetan women it is hard to understand. So, yes, I live here with my second brother and my mother. We look after her since her son, my oldest brother, passed away. And my oldest brother's son is living here too: my nephew. So we are four.

It was my second brother's idea to enclose the upper part of the house. We thought it was too windy. Then some years ago, I told him that it was too cold in the courtyard, so he enclosed that as well. So now we just have the backside to enclose. At first, I was afraid of the glass falling down. And I thought maybe it would be too hot in the summer. But my brother told me that there was a new material that was heatproof, and also that it would not fall. It is not really glass. It is called FRP [fibreglass reinforced polyester]. It is a combination of glass and plastic.

In fact, the glass houses started when I was a kid. People would invite builders to come, sometimes from quite far. Now it is much easier. We go to the city and order; they calculate the area and we pay. When I spoke to the contractor about covering the back side, he said we had to pay for 100 square meters. I called my brother to see how they made this calculation. Then they came and measured the house again and told me that the floor area is 70 square meters and the glass wall is 30. One square meter is 100 yuan; so 100 square meters is over 10,000 yuan. This is very expensive. Before, we built the primary frame ourselves and then we invited the contractors to come and fill in the glass windows.

Our goal in life is to build a house like a palace. Or at least, we want to build a comfortable house. We have to die in a good house. This is the Tibetan understanding of life. The rich ones will rebuild a house after 12 years. It is a waste of money, but they don't care. They just want to build the most fashionable houses.

The older traditional Tibetan houses are quite different. They have two floors. The ground floor is for the animals. It was a kind of barn for the cows. We used to collect the leaves and grass and put them in there for the animals to sleep. Or when it is cold, we put another layer. Then we would use their dung as fertilizer in the fields. I think it is a form of killing if we keep the cows. I could not sleep after we sold the ones we had. I was worried that they would die in a very bad way. So, I just don't raise animals anymore.

We didn't have a kitchen. We did everything on the floor above. We boiled water for cooking, and made food to feed the cows. We didn't have a fridge when we were young. We cut the vegetables in the same room and water was stored in a vat. If the tap ran out, we could use the stored water. Upstairs from the main floor, we used for storage. We stored highland barley and oilseed rapes. We harvested the plants and made them into grains. From the rapes, we made oil. But this year we didn't grow barley because there were not enough people to do the farming. My brother doesn't have time and my mother and I cannot drive the tractor.

He suggested I learn to drive, but for that I would also have to learn how to write and answer the questions. But they will help us with that. My brother said this way I could drive his car to Chengdu to buy clothes for the winter. But I didn't learn because I think it is pointless. I can still catch the bus. And now our neighbor bought a car, so I can go with her.

My mother married when she was in the village. She didn't go to school. But my siblings learned many different things. The oldest learned how to work; and my second brother studied. When I was a kid, we got our first television. We thought it was the most perfect thing in the world. We watched until midnight. We were obsessed with television and didn't study. I always told my brother that if he studied hard he would go to university or become a doctor or teacher. But when the TV arrived I asked him to watch with us. Now he doesn't even have time to make a phone call, my brother. He is very hardworking.

My biggest regret is that I didn't study hard. When I was in second grade I was not good at math. My Chinese was very good. I could finish my recitation homework in three hours. My teacher lived next to the school. The school was next to Songzanlin, not far from here.

When we were kids, my family was poor. My parents didn't grow any vegetables to sell at the time. They just farmed to feed themselves. They did not have time to make money. We cut the wood by ourselves when we built houses as well. In the winter I collected mushrooms in the mountains. I slipped once and broke my bones twice. In 2013 I broke my leg. I stayed home for seven months and we only had a doctor of traditional Chinese medicine nearby. My brother didn't want to bring me there. I asked the doctor how much time it would take to heal, and he said it would take five months. After seven months I could barely walk. I really wanted to die at that time. I also thought if I asked someone for help, I would owe them something. In villages everyone has to do farm work to make money, and if you cannot walk, you cannot make money. And I did not want to use a walking stick. Then my brother brought me to the hospital, and I saw the crack of my bone after I took the CT Scan. People say this kind of crack takes only half a month to heal, but my leg took seven months.

Today there are not so many people still doing farming. It does not pay well. But we are afraid that the government will ask us to return to the land because we are villagers. They bring us together and hold conferences about enhancing our life quality. They tell us to farm and work in tourism. They think Tibetan women buy a lot of gold and tell us instead we should save money for our kids. When we have these government conferences, we get to know each other's full names. Otherwise, we just call each other sister and brother. Few people know my true name. We refer to each other like this since we were kids.

Anyway, no matter how hardworking you are, if your kid is not hardworking, it doesn't make sense. My nephews and nieces understand me. They say I don't have to save money for them. They say they will make their own. I always tell my nephews if you want to live a life like me, that they just have to look at me. If they want to live a life like my second brother, they should look at him.

My niece is at university in Kunming. She called me a few days ago saying she wants to continue with a masters degree. She said her roommate was very rich and selfish, but she could not move to another room. She said it was like hell living with her. I said: "You are not marrying her. So it is ok."

I used to teach her before she started school. When she started, she was a good student because I taught her a lot already. She speaks Putonghua and English. She is not willing to speak Tibetan. She will stay in Kunming for the holidays. I told her not to stay up too late. I don't stay up.

The House Builder, near Xianggelila, Yunnan province, January 2018.

Our village has a lot of glass houses. It is very windy here in the winter and people —tourists—don't come so often. Our house is now very different from before. Upstairs, we used to store fodder for the cows. And we lived on the middle floor. Below was for the livestock. Now it is more comfortable. Everything is different. The storage is all outside and the house is only for living. I transformed the upper floor into a living room. We grow a lot of galsang flowers nearby. When we have guests, I invite them upstairs to view the meadow with the flowers in the summer. It is very beautiful. You can also see the airport. We also will serve dinner there sometimes. Right now we are building a chimney stove. When we finish, we can also cook. For now, it is not possible to sleep upstairs. At night, the winds pick-up and the room is not properly closed from the outside.

I have been building the house for nine years. We were not able to get the wood nearby, so we had to buy it bit by bit from other places. More and more, finding the timber is a big problem. We are not allowed to harvest lumber ourselves locally, so we have to buy timber elsewhere. I bought the wood for the house in Myanmar. It was very expensive. We had to pay even for the elements that we were not able to use. In the past, we would build with rammed-earth walls. But that has also become too expensive. We are not able to find mud locally, as with timber. The government will not allow us to dig into the earth. A concrete wall is cheaper and easier to build.

My family is not very rich. Often I had to support the construction on my own. But that is the tradition here. We build houses when we see that other people have beautiful houses. Even when we die, our children keep on building. This is our tradition, and we don't have another solution. Even when people are rich they still do this. They put millions of yuan into building their houses. I don't think this makes much sense. My parents and my grandfather built their houses and passed them on to me. But I cannot live in them. I still must build my own. And I will pass on my house to my son, but he will also still build his own.

In considering the documentation of the houses that are a part of this book, we returned often to their stories, or narratives; narrative implying an ordered telling that at once constructs and reflects a certain logic. The time of a narrative can move forward or backward, and always comprises the juxtaposition of at least two temporalities: that which is unfolding in the story being told and the time of its telling. This temporal juxtaposition contributes to the articulation of the narrative's logic and its legibility. Within architecture, "narrative" is also used to describe a construction of meaning through the assemblage of material, cultural, and social significations: of a site, project, or design. As with all storytellers, the credibility of an architectural narrator can be compromised.

In *As Found Houses*, we construct narratives through the overlay of descriptions of selected houses with the voices of people whose lives are implicated within them. The narratives of the houses were discerned through site visits, photography, and drawings; of the people through discussions and interviews. By combining the two, it was possible to gain an understanding of the architecture of the houses and their transformations: for example, how a change in family structure led to an addition onto a house, or when accessibility to labor made certain building decisions possible. The record of each house's adaptations could be understood as the manifestation of the residents' histories, their shifting lives mapped onto the architecture itself. In some parts of the world, it is unusual for a lifetime to be lived within a single house, but many of the houses documented in this book were made and cared for by a single generation, or one family over a longer duration. They are family houses, built by the people who live in them.

These material and human histories comprise a text that operates in a reciprocal relation with cultural, social, and economic contexts. Some interviews provide anecdotal support for empirical findings from social science on rural transformation. Other times, those findings explain the material changes that we observed in house construction. While there are many macro-narratives of rural transformation China, the story that became important for us concerned a retelling of vernacular architecture. This narrative was articulated through the observation of self-built adaptations to traditional typologies. The dynamic and contingent quality of these houses challenges an understanding of the vernacular that is staid or of the past. The accelerated speed of contemporary China's transformation has rendered them visible, amplifying the legibility of changes that have been going on for centuries, hidden by duration.

Where past research into these architectures turned most often to well-preserved case studies, we looked instead for houses that were disfigured and adultered: houses that deviated from historical modes of building to propose new hybrid relationships between material, space, and program. To do this, we systematically avoided villages that were known tourist destinations, or, on the other hand, were remote and difficult to access. Instead, we followed recently built, well-traveled, local roads or looked for sites close to regional towns. In these less isolated communities, builders more freely propose new ideas and have easy access to materials and labor. The process of change is accelerated. These new constructions—by local self-builders looking to fulfill specific needs—proliferate throughout the countryside, their value unremarked. But it was exactly these houses that we sought to learn more about.

In this way of looking for and learning from the ordinary, the work enters into a dialogue with "architectural ethnography" as articulated by Momoyo Kaijima and Yoshiharu Tsukamoto of Atelier Bow-Wow since the late 1990s. Architectural ethnography builds on a tradition of research in Japan that foregrounds the observation and documentation of architecture as part of a larger network of human and ecological relations. In 2001, Kaijima and Tsukamoto elaborated on this approach in their search for *da-me* and "Pet" architecture in *Made in Tokyo*. They argued that these spatial categories were inherent to the urbanity of Tokyo, but because of their idiosyncratic specificity, did not register within normative urban readings. Fieldwork—conceived as an embedded, long-term implication with a site and community—was a critical tool. Walks in Tokyo over many years became the primary driver of documentation. These peregrinations made it possible to have a continuous discussion with the urban landscape, looking for unnoticed aspects of the city. The early studies of Tokyo led to more recent investigations of ecological and human processes within rural villages, suburban landscapes, and seaside towns.

Ethnography itself has often studied these processes. Where *architectural* ethnography differs is in its insistent and intensive use of drawing as a form of documentation. Drawing is operative within architectural ethnography both as a process and as an output of that process, as a verb describing an action and its nominative object. As documents, drawings can function through established codes of architectural representation, or innovated notations. They can measure material, tectonic, and spatial relations, or make visible qualities of time, growth, or change. These processes, in turn, articulate social and economic forces in ways that often surpass language alone. While an ethnographic study of vernacular adaptations to rural housing could function entirely without them, drawings deploy a mode of interrogation and construct an articulation of knowledge that is specifically architectural. Drawings, as an outcome of ethnographic observation, are scientific objects of social engagement.

Through the axonometric drawings of *As Found Houses* we wanted to convey a certain immediacy about the houses that comprised a direct and instant apprehension of their qualities. This immediacy relates to the accessibility of the axonometric as a mode of architectural drawing. The axonometries render the houses into discrete objects of study. They make visible specific readings of the spatial, constructive or material facts, such that the houses each become legible characters. Each character then enters into a relation with other aspects of the research that describe the contingent conditions that led to its articulation. Within the context of a proliferation of hybrid construction in the Chinese countryside—and the acceleration of changes to the rural—the legibility of the axonometries and the immediacy they proffer carries the weight of the narratives that are told within the book.

The plan drawings address a longer time-space. In part, they try to communicate the ideal, typological origin that informs each of the houses. This origin can both constrain and allow variation. It can be made more legible through the process of transformation or recede and disappear into a latent condition. The challenge within the drawings was to create an oscillation between recent design decisions linked to program, materials, and construction and the more embedded condition of typology. In the smaller houses—the wooden and underground—we draw furniture and objects to describe the new ways in which families appropriate the spaces of their houses; these modes of living are sometimes linked to the additions and alterations they have made. They can also be clues to how the houses could change in the future.

The axonometry and plan drawings that describe each house are derived from measurements, photographs, and notes taken during fieldwork—a process familiar to any architect confronted with a new project. The effort of carefully recording existing conditions at a given site provides information and insight for the future. Nevertheless, measurements and photographs invariably produce an incomplete record, such that drawing becomes an informed extrapolation from those facts that are better understood. The process of drawing an existing structure also calls for an empathetic projection into the mind of the earlier builder or architect, into their decisions and logic. Drawing and re-drawing lines become a kind of excavation into this thinking that simultaneously develops the sensibility of the one who is re-drawing: clarifying the present through the past and binding the architect in a specifically architectural way—through drawing—to what they are studying.

Essential to ethnography is its self-reflexive questioning of the link between subject and researcher. This link can be mutually influencing, such that both researcher and subject are affected and transformed by observation. Observation, regardless of whether it is active or passive, transforms the subject. Reciprocally, observation also influences the researcher who changes through the experience of the work. In architectural ethnography, we could argue that this process of mutual influence operates upon drawing as well as the researcher. An architect drawing what they see transforms the tools of their practice. The close observation of the worlds being studied becomes a resource for thinking about architecture. Research, in this sense, ultimately influences design. In trying to understand a phenomenon outside of ourselves through drawing, the architect is able to instrumentalize the research at its origins.

In his 1995 essay, "The Artist as Ethnographer," Hal Foster describes a wariness about an ethnographic turn in art. This shift in practice and exhibition comprised artists who used fieldwork within marginalized communities to identify transgressive social or cultural practices that would become a resource for making artworks. These found communities were marginal in the sense of being outside of the mainstream, either physically removed and remote or outcast through other forms of distancing.

The artist, Foster argues, refashions these communities and their experience into a reconstituted representation destined for the gallery or museum. He describes "a vogue for pseudoethnographic reports in art that are sometimes disguised travelogues from the world art market[,]" and asks: "Who in the academy or the art world has not witnessed these new forms of *flanerie*?" The turn toward ethnography was motivated by envy toward the discipline as a perceived "science of alterity" that was able to take culture as its object while also embedding itself into local contexts through fieldwork. Ethnography also invited self-critique through its reflexive need to consider the subject-researcher relationship as well as other disciplinary methodologies and objectives.

In Foster's art-world, the artist reconstitutes his practice through the authority of the *other*, such that research into the ethnographic subject ultimately circles back into the figure of the artist who remains at the center. Attempts to situate this cycle within collaborative processes or as destabilizations of political agency were undermined by their institutional context within galleries or museums that were part of larger systems of exclusion. Foster is writing about a specific moment in time within a circumscribed world of art practices, but his caution could also be turned toward architectural ethnography.

Is the art-world *flaneur* that Foster describes no different from the architectural tourist? Does architectural ethnography simply produce "disguised travelogues" without the reflexive criticality that characterizes and constitutes ethnography as a discipline? Books that have been influential for us, such as *Architecture without Architects* or *Learning from Las Vegas*, are deeply rooted within the discipline's arms-length relationship with tourism, at once partaking in its opportunities, but asserting a critical distance in the name of research. *Made in Tokyo* is itself fashioned as a guide-book for the *other* Tokyo: the city as it is never depicted within regular tourist publications. And architectural ethnography, in its engagement not only with the built environment but also with communities, enters into a terrain that makes Foster's questions even more relevant. Is it possible for architecture to adopt ethnographic methods that foreground the human realm in a way that doesn't Instrumentalize those subjects and simply re-inscribe the architect's expertise?

The interviews that appear in this book are narrative overlays onto the drawings. If drawing offers a tool for looking at the houses that is specifically architectural, the interviews with residents, builders, and villagers adopt a method that is more closely linked to ethnography. These discussions were recorded, transcribed, and translated from Mandarin dialects into English, edited into first-person accounts, anonymized, and edited again. The interview texts are several times removed from the words that were spoken. This string of mediations between what was uttered and what appears makes their constructed nature explicit. The winding stories that result do not always touch on the houses and most do not refer directly to them.

The photographs of the houses function as documentary evidence. While some were taken to provide a record that could be used later, others were shot with the objective of transmitting specific information. They most often stand alone on their pages within the book, offering a quality of space, material, and place that other forms of documentation are less capable of conveying. In this sense, they straddle the dual functions of affirming a certain veracity and describing ineffable qualities that are beyond verification.

We identify each house with a descriptive name instead of through a geographic location—for example the village where they are situated. Through the name, the character described with the axonometric drawing is made explicit. The names frame a specific spatial or programmatic reading of their transformation while also generalizing the houses with this reduction. The naming provokes a reconsideration of the proliferation of adapted houses through the specificity of the strategies of self-builders. The houses can be found everywhere in the countryside, yet each house is a singular character. In naming them, we argue for the value of the transformations as acts of architecture.

The drawings, photographs, interviews, and texts function analytically in their articulation of possible narratives. They are descriptive elements that reflect readings of the houses we encountered and judgments about what was important in each. The book functions through the space opened up by the juxtaposition of these descriptive layers. That space is at once delimited and potential, open to other possible readings. Juxtaposition can render such a space when each descriptive element maintains a certain autonomy. In this sense, the drawings are complete in themselves, while still in dialogue with each other. Each photo is a story of its own. And the interviews, despite the steps mediating their reception, present the villagers' voices in ways that surpass the frame of the book.

The force of narratives that occupy such a space, at once delimited and potential, I would argue, lies in their irresoluble quality, in the way they can oscillate between a singular telling and other retellings. This value is qualified not by narrative hold over a subject, but rather by the ability to sustain and disperse resonances, thus returning a degree of autonomy to that subject. In this way, the houses in this book remain to be found.

What, for us, has been meaningful is how they so unexpectedly manifest architecture's capacity to both register and enact changes to ways of living, and to the world.

ACKNOWLEDGMENTS

A team of architects and student researchers helped make this book possible. We are grateful for their efforts and always keen eyes.

RESEARCH LEADER
Eva Herunter

RESEARCHERS
Rebekka Hirschberg
Xia Chengwei

TRANSLATION
Liu Chang

RESEARCH ASSISTANTS
Chan Yuen Shing Finn
Cheung Wai-Lun Vernon
Cheung Yui Ming
Chung Bing Tsun Lester
Phoebe Cowen
Fan Xinkai
Bo Yee Lau
Lin Yingying
Lu Sixiao
Chiara Oggioni
Josephine Saabye
Shen Yifan
Sun Yi
Haotian Zhang

FUNDING

The research at the origin of *As Found Houses* was funded by the University Grants Committee General Research Fund of the Hong Kong SAR government.

A grant from the design publishing fund of the Department of Architecture, University of Hong Kong, helped with the production of the book.

The Faculty of Architecture, through its support of the Rural Urban Framework, facilitated investigations that are at the project's origin and the lab structure that served as home to the research.

AS FOUND HOUSES

IMAGE CREDITS

Page 6, by Graf zu Castell-Rüdenhausen. Used with the permission of the copyright holder.

All other images were taken as part of the research.

IMPRINT

Published by Applied Research and Design Publishing, an imprint of ORO Editions.
Gordon Goff: Publisher

www.appliedresearchanddesign.com
info@appliedresearchanddesign.com

AUTHORS
John Lin and Sony Devabhaktuni

CONTRIBUTORS
Yung Ho Chang

GRAPHIC DESIGN
Studio Otamendi (Manuela Dechamps Otamendi assisted by Laurine Tribolet and Benny Ouioui)

COVER DESIGN
Chiara Oggioni and Haotian Zhang

COPY-EDITING ASSISTANCE
Rebecca Reading

PROOFREADING
Phoebe Cowen

PROJECT MANAGER
Jake Anderson

LITHOGRAPHY
Mistral (Olivier Dengis)

COLOR SEPARATIONS AND PRINTING
ORO Group Ltd.
Printed in China.

AR+D Publishing makes a continuous effort to minimize the overall carbon footprint of its publications. As part of this goal, AR+D, in association with Global ReLeaf, arranges to plant trees to replace those used in the manufacturing of the paper produced for its books. Global ReLeaf is an international campaign run by American Forests, one of the world's oldest nonprofit conservation organizations. Global ReLeaf is American Forests' education and action program that helps individuals, organizations, agencies, and corporations improve the local and global environment by planting and caring for trees.

10 9 8 7 6 5 4 3 2 First Edition

ISBN: 978-1-943532-79-7